Something Torn and New

SOMETHING TORN AND NEW

An African Renaissance

Ngũgĩ wa Thiong'o

BASIC
CIVITAS
BOOKS

A MEMBER OF THE PERSEUS BOOKS GROUP
NEW YORK

Books published by BasicCivitas Books are available at
special discounts for bulk purchases in the United States
by corporations, institutions, and other organizations. For
more information, please contact the Special Markets
Department at the Perseus Books Group, 2300 Chestnut
Street, Suite 200, Philadelphia, PA 19103, or call (800)
810-4145, ext. 5000, or e-mail
special.markets@perseusbooks.com.

Designed by Timm Bryson

Library of Congress Cataloging-in-Publication Data
Ngugi wa Thiong'o, 1938–
   Something torn and new : an African renaissance / Ngugi
wa Thiong'o.
      p. cm.
   Includes bibliographical references and index.
   ISBN 978-0-465-00946-6 (alk. paper)
   1. Africa—Civilization. 2. Decolonization—Africa. I.
Title.

   DT14.N48 2008
   325.6—dc22

                              2008044278

10 9 8 7 6 5 4 3 2 1

For Sonia Sanchez, Amiri Baraka, Ntongela Masilela,
Haunani-Kay Trask, Michael Neill,
Tim Reiss, and Pat Hilden

And in memory of the late Ngũgĩ wa Mĩriĩ,
Apollo Njonjo, Kĩmani Roki, and Ime Ikiddeh

CONTENTS

PREFACE

When in 2002 I accepted Professor Henry Louis ("Skip") Gates's invitation to give the 2006 McMillan-Stewart Lectures at Harvard, I had no particular subject in mind. The germ of the theme of memory and renaissance that now runs through this book was originally expressed in the 2003 Biko Memorial Lecture (currently Chapter 4), that I gave at the University of Cape Town, South Africa. I took up the same theme in my acceptance speech for the Honorary PhD of Philosophy and Literature awarded me by the Albert Sisulu University in South Africa in 2004. At the time, it was becoming clear to me that the question of memory may not only explain what ails contemporary Africa but may also contain the seeds of communal renewal and self-confidence.

This idea eventually crystallized into a phrase, *Re-membering Africa,* which became the title of the Nairobi-based Ford Foundation lecture that I gave at the University of Nairobi at

Kenya and the University of Dar-es-Salaam at Tanzania in July 2004, to mark my return to Kenya after twenty-two years in exile. An account of the lecture occupied the front page of English- and Kiswahili-language newspapers with sensational headlines like *"Africa Is Headed by Wrong Heads, Ngūgĩ Says."* I gave the lecture for the last time at my *alma mater*, Makerere University at Kampala, on August 10, 2004. That evening, at midnight, after I had returned to Nairobi, Kenya, hired gunmen broke into my apartment two blocks from the Central Police Station and brutally attacked my wife and me. These men stole the computer that contained the lecture, the only major item taken. We narrowly escaped death. By this time, the theme of the Harvard lectures had become quite apparent to me.

The first three chapters of this book originated as the McMillan-Stewart Lectures, which I delivered at the Dubois Institute of African and African-American Studies in March 2006 and at the University of Nairobi in January 2007 as part of the East African Educational Publishers' launch of the Kenyan edition of my novel, *Wizard of the Crow*. These lectures contain my thinking on the decolonization of African memory. It was astonishing to discover, in writing them, the centrality of the Irish experience to the colonial question, especially as it relates to language, culture, and social memory. Ireland was England's first colony, and it became a prototype for all other English colonies in Asia, Africa, and America. Irish missionaries, army officers, and administrative officials were often considered part of the British empire, thus possibly explaining why Rudyard Kipling chose to make Kim, the eponymous hero of his novel, both Irish and working class, as if to show that both the British proletariat and the colonized alike were willing servants of the empire. Anglo-Irish literature was certainly used in the service of the cultural self-image of the empire: It was an integral component of the English canon in schools and colleges in Africa, often taught as the empire's "gift to the world." But the colonial context of the Irish writers' texts was erased from their artistic being. The European Renaissance also figures strongly in this book. The capitalist modernity to which it gave birth cannot be divorced from the colonial moment it came into being.

There is no region, no culture, no nation today that has not been affected by colonialism and its aftermath. Indeed, modernity can be considered a product of colonialism. This book speaks to the decolonization of modernity.

CHAPTER ONE

DISMEMBERING PRACTICES

Planting European Memory in Africa[1]

Waiyaki wa Hinga, sometimes called simply Waiyaki, is one
of the most important figures in Agĩkũyũ anticolonial resistance lore. One of the leaders of the nineteenth-century resistance against the British military occupation, he harassed
British forces time and again. In particular, he attacked Fort
Smith in Dagoretti after the British broke the peace treaty he
had agreed to in talks with the British colonial agent, Captain
Lugard. When they finally captured him, the British removed
Waiyaki from his region, the base of his power, and, on the
way to the Kenya Coast, buried him alive at Kibwezi, head
facing the bowels of the earth—in opposition to the Gĩkũyũ
burial rites' requirement that the body face Mount Kenya, the
dwelling place of the Supreme Deity. Similarly, in Xhosaland,
the present-day Eastern Cape of South Africa, the British

captured King Hintsa of the Xhosa resistance and decapitated him, taking his head to the British Museum, just as they had done with the decapitated head of the Maori King of New Zealand.

The relationship between Africa and Europe is well represented by the fate of these figures. A colonial act—indeed, any act in the context of conquest and domination—is both a practice of power, intended to pacify a populace, and a symbolic act, a performance of power intended to produce docile minds. The lynching of captive Africans in the American South, often accompanied by the brutal removal and public display of their genitalia—the strange fruits borne by Southern trees that Billie Holiday sang about—was likewise meant to instill fear and compliant docility.

In 1900, Sir Fredrick Hodgson, a British colonial governor in what was then the Gold Coast, demanded the surrender of the *Sika'dwa* (Golden Stool)—the embodiment of the Ashanti *sunsum* (soul) and symbol of their nationhood—so that he might sit on it, thereby triggering the great Ashanti anticolonial resistance led by Asantehene Yaa-Asantewaa. Similarly, Cecil Rhodes wanted to be buried in the mountains, the sacred burial sites of the Kings of the Matabele of Zimbabwe. The symbolism of these demands was not subtle: Both were acts of triumph and humiliation. But the beheading of King Hintsa and the burial of Waiyaki alive, body upside down, and the removal of the genitalia of the Africans in America, go beyond particular acts of conquest and humiliation: They are enactments of the central character of colonial practice in general and of Europe's contact with Africa in particular since the beginnings of capitalist modernity and bourgeois ascendancy. This contact is characterized by dismemberment. An act of absolute social engineering, the continent's dismemberment was simultaneously the foundation, fuel, and consequence of Europe's capitalist modernity.

The dismemberment of Africa occurred in two stages. During the first of these, the African personhood was divided into two halves: the continent and its diaspora. African slaves, the central commodity in the mercantile phase of capitalism, formed the basis of the sugar, cotton, and tobacco plantations in the Caribbean and American mainland. If we accept that slave trade and plantation slavery provided the primary accumulation of capital that made Europe's Industrial Revolution possible,[2] we cannot escape the irony that the very needs of that Industrial Revolution—markets for finished goods, sources of raw materials, and strategic requirements in the defense of trade routes—led inexorably to the second stage of the dismemberment of the continent.

The Berlin Conference of 1884 literally fragmented and reconstituted Africa into British, French, Portuguese, German, Belgian, and Spanish Africa. Just as the slave plantations were owned by various European powers, so post–Berlin Conference Africa was transformed into a series of colonial plantations owned by many of the same European powers.

The requirements of the slave plantation demanded the physical removal of human resources from the continent to work on land stolen from other subject peoples, mainly native Caribbeans and native Americans. The result was an additional dismemberment of the diasporic African, who was now separated not only from his continent and his labor but also from his very sovereign being. The subsequent colonial plantations on the African continent have led to the same result: division of the African from his land, body, and mind. The land is taken away from its owner, and the owner is turned into a worker on the same land, thus losing control of his natural and human resources. The colonial subject has no say over the colonial state; in effect, he produces but has no say over the disposal of the product. Yet the state has power over every aspect of his being. Whereas before he was his own subject, now he is subject to another.

But the fate of Hintsa and Waiyaki also symbolize an even farther-reaching dismemberment: that of the colonial subject's memory from his individual and collective body. The head that carries memory is cut off from the body and then either stored in the British Museum or buried upside down. Joseph Conrad dramatized such acts in the fictional *Heart of*

Darkness, where the skulls of slain Africans decorate the walls
of the Belgian colonial despot. The reality, as documented by
Roger Casement and satirized by Mark Twain, was no less
gruesome.

Of course, colonialists did not literally cut off the heads of
the colonized or physically bury them alive. Rather, they dismembered the colonized from memory, turning their heads
upside down and burying all the memories they carried.

Wherever they went, in their voyages of land, sea, and
mind, Europeans planted their own memories on whatever
they contacted. In his book *The Idea of Africa,* V. Y. Mudimbe
writes, "The geographic expansion of Europe and its civilization . . . submitted the world to its memory."[3] Mapping, which
involves exploration and surveying, was followed first by naming and then by ownership. Mapping was the imperial road to
power and domination. The fictive figure of Christopher Marlowe's Tamburlaine comes to mind. Even in his last gasps of
breath, Tamburlaine is still hankering after a map:

> *Give me a map; then let me see how much*
> *Is left for me to conquer all the world, . . .*[4]

A map in his hands, the world left for him to conquer includes
Egypt, Arabia, India, Nubia, Ethiopia, and across the tropical
line to Zanzibar, then north until he has all of Africa under his

sword. The imaginary Tamburlaine dies before he can achieve world domination—he does not even know America exists, but his real-life historical children do know and carry on his renaissance ambitions of mapping, naming, and owning.

Columbus goes west across the Atlantic and, despite finding people inhabiting the lands, he calls the region he finds there "New Hispaniola." Later the whole landmass is named America after Amerigo Vespucci. Much later we get New York, New Jersey, New Britain, New Haven, and of course New England. Maori territory, Aotearoa, becomes New Zealand. An entire Asian/Pacific landscape becomes the Philippines. Africa is no different. The African landscape is blanketed with European memory of place. Names like Port Elisabeth, King Williamstown, Queenstown, and Grahamstown cover the landscape that Hintsa died protecting from foreign occupation. Westlands (formerly Kīrūngiī) and Karen now become the names of the lands Waiyaki once traversed. Lake East Africa, the main source of the River Nile and hence the base of one of the major world civilizations, is named for Victoria. But all these places had names before—names that pointed to other memories, older memories. To the Luo people of Kenya, Lake East Africa was known as Namlolwe. A European memory becomes the new marker of geographical identity, covering up an older memory or, more strictly speaking, burying the native memory of place. Now and then, as in the case of New Zealand and even America, one can see the older and newer memories in contention with place names; but generally after the planting of European memory, the identity of place becomes that of Europe. Even today, years after achievement of political independence, the African continent is often identified as Anglophone, Francophone, or Lusaphone.

Europe has also planted its memory on the bodies of the colonized. This phenomenon is not peculiarly European but, rather, is in the nature of all colonial conquests and systems of foreign occupation. In his attempt to remake the land and its peoples in his image, the conqueror acquires and asserts the right to name the land and its subjects, demanding that the subjugated accept the names and culture of the conqueror. When Japan occupied Korea in 1906, it banned Korean names and required the colonized to take on Japanese ones. But one might ask: What is in a name? It is said that a rose by any other name would still smell as sweet; however, the truth is that its identity would no longer be expressed in terms of roses but, instead, would assume that of the new name. Names have everything to do with how we identify objects, classify them, and remember them. The encounter between the unnamed man and Crusoe in Defoe's *Robinson Crusoe* readily comes to mind. "... I was greatly delighted with him," says Crusoe, "and made it my business to teach him everything that was proper to make him useful, handy and helpful; but especially to make him speak, and understand me when I spoke; and he was the aptest scholar that ever was...."[5] The education program that Crusoe sets up for the man begins with names. Crusoe does not even bother to ask the man's name: "[A]nd first I let him know that his name should be Friday, which was the day I saved his life; . . . I likewise taught him to say 'Master,' and then let him know that was to be my name."[6] Subject and master become the terms of their exchange. Even simple greetings—How are you, Friday? I am fine, Master—express their unequal relationship. Friday's body no longer carries any memory of previous identity to subvert the imposed identity.

Our next example comes from Edmund Spenser, celebrated author of *The Faerie Queen,* the poetic manual of English nationalism. Spenser is important to Africa because his works were central to the canon of English national literature. As a student of English in Ibadan, Abiola Irele coined the mellifluous phrase *Spenser to Spender,* to describe the English literature syllabus taught in the overseas colleges of the University of London—Achimota in Ghana, Makerere in Uganda, and the University of the West Indies in Mona, Jamaica, and so on. All of these colleges were established in the postwar period when British colonialism, unable to exist according to the old rules, saw the necessity of creating an African middle class for future partnership.

Spenser's personal connection to Irish colonial settlements, his advocacy of the genocidal scorched-earth policy of creating famine to force the Irish to capitulate, and his unabashed nationalism were not of course the focus of the study of his works, *The Faerie Queen* and *The Shephearde's Calendar*. But this focus makes a great deal of sense in our colonial context. For Spenser was not just a poet; he was a colonial official and ideologue of an England consolidating itself into a nation-state, threatened by the rival ideologies of papacy and Spanish nationalism.[7] Most important and formative in his poetry and politics was the fact that he was an English settler in Ireland, in close touch with a culture he loathed and envied, as is made clear in his important prose dialogue, *A View of the Present State of Ireland*.[8] This view is expressed in the form of a Platonic dialogue between a seasoned English colonist in Ireland, Iraenius, and an English gentleman close to the English court, Eudoxus. The two interlocutors represent the two sides of Spenser himself, the Official and the Settler. What they come up with is nothing short of what Laura O'Connor has called a "blueprint for the country's permanent military occupation,"[9] of which the systematic erasure of the Irish memory is a necessary component. Spenser sees abrogation of the Irish naming system, which carries memories of clan, lineage, and place—all implicated in the inducement of amnesia among the colonized. He therefore recommends that this system be decreed:

> That from thenceforth each one should take unto himself a several surname, either of his trade or faculty of some quality of his body or his mind, or of the place where he dwelt, so as every one should be distinguished from the other or from the most part; whereby they shall not only not depend upon the head of their sept as now they do, but also shall in short time learn quite to forget his Irish nation. And therewithal would I also wish all the Oes and the Macs which the heads of the septs have taken to their names to be utterly forbidden and extinguished.[10]

Since the Oes and Macs were made for the strengthening of the Irish identity, "the abrogating thereof will as much enfeeble them."[11] The loss of name, linked to loss of memory, would help break, or at least weaken, the Irish resistance to the English-settler colonization of this "goodly and commodious a soil," as Eudoxus describes Ireland, "turning thereof to good uses, and reducing that savage nation to better government and civility."[12]

The road to colonial hell, at least for the colonized, has always been paved with good intentions. Note that Spenser is horrified by another possibility as well: that the colonial settler might take on the names of the local habitation. Iraenius decries the case of some earlier English settlers who "are degenerate and grown to be as very patchocks as the wild Irish, yea and some of them have quite shaken off the English names and put on Irish, that they might be altogether Irish."[13] To which Eudoxus, the other interlocutor, responds with even greater horror. "Is it possible," he asks, "that any should so far grow out of frame that they should in so short space quite forget their country and their own names?"[14] Yet "out of frame" is exactly how Spenser's literary alter-ego Iraenius wants the Irish to grow when he recommends that they be made to abandon their Oes and Macs.

Spenser's *View* was published in 1586, and no doubt much of it would have been read by those who were devising schemes for the settler colonies in the "new" world. Ireland was the first English colony. Spenser and Sir Walter Raleigh—writer, explorer, spy, colonizer—were of the same circle, both landowners in the Irish province of Munster. The ideas in the *View* were carried by Raleigh and company to America, the settler plantation in Ireland having become the prototype of the English settler plantation in America and the Caribbean. The attitude toward Native Americans was the same as that articulated in the *View* vis-à-vis the Irish.

The experience of the millions of Africans brought in slave ships to America best illustrates Spenser's strategy. A systematic program eliminated their memory of Africa. Their own names and naming systems once again were seen as a barrier to the intended amnesia. So, break up their names. Give them the names of the owners of the plantations to signify their being the property of Brown or Smith or Williams. The English were not alone in carrying out this program, for we find the same story in the French, Dutch, and Spanish zones. It was as if all of them were reading from the same manual. The result was that everyone in the African diaspora, from the tiniest Caribbean and Pacific island to the American mainland, lost their names: Their bodies became branded with a European memory.

This program was reimported into the African continent. The story is told of how Dom Alfonso, Mani Congo, the king of the Congo in the seventeenth century, sent appeals for modern doctors from Portugal. They sent him not doctors but Portuguese names, along with a manual on how to organize his court according to a European feudal model with Portuguese nomenclature.[15] On the heels of the names came Christian zealots, slave traders, and, later, Portuguese settlers.

If the human body has a language—we often talk of body language—it has also been used as a writing surface. Decorations on the body can tell a narrative of clan and place. But the body has also been used to carry messages against itself, as Page DuBois documents in her book *Torture and Truth*.[16]

Slaves, before they left the African shore, were branded with marks of their owners. Theirs, literally, was a baptism by fire. Later, holy water would replace the hot iron: A successful Christian conversion, by force or guile, meant marking the re-formed African body with a European name. Thus, in the nineteenth century, the writing of European names on the bodies of the African convert became the Christian norm. No different from the branded bodies of the enslaved, African bodies carry marks of Europe in the form of names. If the di-aspora resulted in the death of African names, the continent saw the shadowing of African names by European ones. The African body became a walking commercial for European memory, rather reminiscent of T. S. Eliot asking:

> Who is the third who walks always beside you?
> When I count, there are only you and I together
> But when I look ahead up the white road
> There is always another one walking beside you
> Gliding wrapt in a brown mantle, hooded
> I do not know whether a man or a woman
> —But who is that on the other side of you?[17]

Europe also planted its memory on the mind. If the planting of its memory on the body was effected through names, the one on the mind was accomplished through the vast naming system of language. In his recent book *Empires of the Word*, Nicholas Ostler maintains that language is the prime mover in world history. "Far more than princes, states and economies," he writes, "it is language communities who are the real players in world history, persisting through the ages, clearly and consciously perceived by their speakers as symbols of identity, but nonetheless gradually changing, and perhaps splitting or even merging as the communities react to new realities."[18]

In my books *Decolonising the Mind, Moving the Center,* and *Writers in Politics*, I have pointed out the use of language in the deconstruction of a sovereign African and his reconstruction as a colonial subject. When you did not know yourself, I gave you language, Prospero tells Caliban in Shakespeare's *The Tempest.* At this point in the play, Prospero has of course taken the land, after surveying and getting information about the island from Caliban. I was my own subject, now I am yours, curses Caliban, very much aware that he has lost his sovereignty. Prospero's position was likewise articulated, approvingly of course, by the real-life Spenser, in relation to England's first colony, Ireland. Conscious of the critical role of language in the conception of selfhood and otherness, he is dismayed to find that some of the earlier English settlers spoke Irish, for it is "unnatural that any should love another's language more than their own."[19] The English settlers should "take scorn to acquaint their tongues thereto, for it hath been ever the use of the conqueror to despise the language of the conquered, and to force him by all means to learn his."[20] It is terrible to have another's language imposed upon one but acceptable to impose one's language on another. It is the right of the conqueror.

Africans, in the diaspora and on the continent, were soon to be the recipients of this linguistic logic of conquest, with two results: linguicide in the case of the diaspora and linguistic famine, or linguifam, on the continent. Linguicide[21] is the linguistic equivalent of genocide. Genocide involves conscious acts of physical massacre; linguicide, conscious acts of language liquidation. Linguicide, writes Skutnabb-Kanga, "implies that there are agents involved in causing the death of languages."[22] This is precisely the fate of African languages in the diaspora. "The encounter between African Languages (Yoruba, Igbo, Twi, Kikongo, and many others) and Western languages (French, Spanish, Dutch, Portuguese, English) was perhaps the most subtle and most complex aspect of the cultural confrontation that the African slaves faced in the New World,"[23] writes Henry Louis Gates, Jr. "Radically abstracted from their cultural communities, and broadly dispersed from plantation to plantation, state to state, and country to country, the African slaves in much of North America soon lost the capacity to speak their own African languages."[24]

Even the drum was forbidden. "The strictest, most brutal forms of punishment were meted out to those Africans insistent upon retaining their own languages, calling themselves by their true names," continues Gates. Forbidden to use his language, and with the natural nurseries of language, families, and communities constantly broken up and relocated, the new-world African is, over time, disconnected from his linguistic base in the continent. "What we might usefully think of as the Americanization of the slave took place, most directly and forcibly, at the level of language,"[25] writes Gates. The liquidation was clearly and consciously meant to deny slaves their languages both as means of communication and as sites of remembrance and desire. At the same time, the linguistic connection to Europe was reinforced for the Spanish, the Dutch, the French, and the English plantation owners.

On the continent, languages are not liquidated in the same way. What happens to them, in this post–Berlin Conference era of direct colonialism, is linguistic famine. Linguifam is to languages what famine is to the people who speak them— linguistic deprivation and, ultimately, starvation. It is interesting that Spenser, in his manual for colonizing the Irish, also recommends a scorched-earth policy to induce famine. He had seen such a policy break resistance in Munster (as noted, both Spenser and Raleigh had plantations there) where despite previously being endowed with plenty of cattle and corn: "[Y]et ere one year and a half they were brought up to such wretchedness, as that any stony heart would have rued the same. Out of the very corner of the woods and glens they came creeping forth upon their hands, for their legs could not bear them. They looked anatomies of death, they spake like ghosts crying out of their graves."[26] Two and a half centuries later, following the English-induced potato famine of 1846–1860, during which Irish people died in large numbers and many survivors were forced to emigrate to America, the weakened community that remained was unable to resist linguistic Anglicization through new education policies that imposed English on the Irish. In the African continent, African languages—deprived of the food, water, light, and oxygen of thought, and of the constant conceptualizing that facilitates forging of the new and renewal of the old—underwent slow starvation, linguifam. Whereas before they were robust languages—the languages spoken by those who built ancient Egypt, Timbuctoo, Zimbabwe, Malindi, Mombasa, and Mogandishu, cities cited by Milton in *Paradise Lost* as those of the future, when the Angel Michael takes Adam to the top of the highest hill before expulsion from paradise (yes, even the languages of the ancient civilizations of Ghana, Mali, Sudan, and Mwenematope)—slightly over a century and a half of colonial contact with Europe turned them into ghosts from graveyards over which now lie European linguistic plantations.

Language is a communication system and carrier of culture by virtue of being simultaneously the means and carrier
of memory—what Frantz Fanon calls "bearing the weight of
a civilization."[27] What Walter Benjamin says of memory, that
it "is not an instrument for exploring the past, but rather a
medium,"[28] is also true of language vis-à-vis memory: Language is the clarifying medium of memory or rather the two
are intertwined. To starve or kill a language is to starve and
kill a people's memory bank. And it is equally true that to impose a language is to impose the weight of experience it carries and its conception of self and otherness—indeed, the
weight of its memory, which includes religion and education.

Spenser, through his literary alter-ego Iraenius, has a clear
idea of what he wants religion and education to achieve
among his colonial targets. In particular, he recommends
that a petty schoolteacher be adjoined to the parish church,
"which should bring up their children in the first rudiments
of letters; and that in every country or baronry they should
keep an able schoolmaster, which should instruct them in
grammar and in the principles of sciences, to whom they
should be compelled to send their youth to be disciplined,
whereby they will in short time grow up to that civil conversation, that both the children will loathe the former rudeness
in which they were bred, and also their parents will, even by
the ensample of their young children, perceive the foulness

of their own brutish behaviour compared to theirs, for learning hath that wonderful power of itself that it can soften and
temper the most stern and savage nature."[29]

In his celebrated novel *Ambiguous Adventure*, Cheikh
Hamidou Kane notes that the cannon and the new colonial
school went hand in hand in the subjugation of the colonized.
In fact, as if borrowing from Spenser, he credits the school as
possessing more power than the cannon for "better than the
cannon it made conquest permanent. The cannon compels
the body and the school bewitches the soul."[30]

Language, religion, and education are to be deployed to
achieve loss of memory and dismember the Irish elite from
their parental social body. The idea, as clearly articulated by
Spenser, is to construct an elite who shall carry the weight of
the colonizer's memory and become the means by which the
elite's parents shall lose cultural memory. Years later in India,
another of the early English colonies, an educator, Lord
Macaulay, would recommend the same Spenserian dispen-
sation to bring up, through English language and literature, "a
class of persons, Indians in blood and colour, but English in
taste, in opinions, in morals and in intellect,"[31] to act as the
middlemen between the English and the millions of Indians
they governed. Get a few of the natives, empty their hard disk
of previous memory, and download into them a software of
European memory. The colonizer's memory sees nothing but

savagery and barbarism when it contemplates the land, the body, the culture, and the language of the people it wants to colonize, be they Maoris, Native Americans, Africans, Asians, or even other European peoples. This propensity is more sharply accentuated in situations where the colonizer and colonized represent not just two religions—Catholicism and Protestantism, for instance, as in the case of Ireland— but also two contrasting skin pigments, as in the case of Africa.

When Europe contemplated Africa through the prism of its bourgeois desire to conquer and dominate, it saw nothing but uninhabited lands. A uniform rationale for European settlements in Kenya, Zimbabwe, and South Africa was that the land was empty of human beings. Where inhabited, it was by hordes of savages virtually indistinguishable from nature— an integral part of the gloom that Conrad depicted in *Heart of Darkness*, contact with which could cause a fairly enlightened European to degenerate into primitivity. Bourgeois memory of Africa removes all traces of human imprints on the land: It becomes untamed, part of what Hegel termed "unconscious nature." When any part of the continent exhibits marks that might compare favorably with Europe, it is "yanked" from Africa, or at least from writings about the region. Note, for instance, the difference between premodern and modern European views of Africa. To Pliny it was an Africa out of which comes something new, even though he believed "the new" was mostly grotesque, whereas post-Renaissance Europe, particularly during the nineteenth century, has seen it as darkness. Or as W.E.B. Dubois put it in 1915: "The medieaval European world knew the Blackman chiefly as a legend or occasional curiosity, but still as a fellow man—an Othello, a Prester John, or an Antar. The modern world, in contrast, knows the Negro chiefly as a bond slave in the West Indies and America . . . and we face today throughout the dominant world [the belief] that color is a mark of inferiority."[32] To bear out Dubois, we can turn to no less an authority than Hegel, who, in his lectures on the philosophy of history, described Africa as having no history for it was still enveloped in the dark mantle of the night. History as the march of freedom and reason had bypassed the dark continent. The degree to which these views had become normalized in the European intellectual conception of the continent is made clear by the fact that as late as 1960, when many countries in Africa were regaining some measure of their sovereignty, Trevor Roper of Oxford University could still advance Hegel's perspective as an obvious one that needed no proof when he talked of Africa as being in total darkness prior to the European presence—and darkness, of course, could never be a subject of history. The unmistakable conclusion was that Africa entered history only through its colonization by Europe. And what of Egypt? Or North Africa—Carthage, in particular? No problem for Hegel and his followers: That was not Africa at all, but part of the Mediterranean—what he called "European Africa."

And even with respect to contemplation of the body itself, blackness was seen as necessary for the self-contemplation of whiteness. Europe was lightness as opposed to benighted blackness. The enlightenment of Hume, Kant, and Hegel was affirmed by its opposite. Their philosophy—developing as it did in the context of slavery, through explorer narratives of the dark continent and missionary accounts—embraced the darkness of otherness, and that's why the African philosopher Emmanuel Chukwudi Eze has so aptly criticized their racialized philosophy in terms of color of reason. Rationality wore the color of white. Whiteness was the desirable human norm. We can see this in the white performance of blackness, for evidence of which, in turn, we might as well go back to the beginnings of capitalist modernity.

Ben Jonson, a contemporary of both Shakespeare and Spenser, began his genre of court masques (he wrote more than sixty) with the *Masque of Blackness*, in which twelve daughters of Niger, previously at ease with their bodies and themselves, awaken to their "ugliness" after hearing of distant whiteness. They are so completely dissatisfied with their skin color that they daily pester their Father Niger to seek a cure:

> *They wept such ceaseless tears into my stream*
> *That it has thus far overflowed his shore.*[33]

Their hope for deliverance lies in a journey to a Land called Britannia, where "Their beauties shall be scorched no more," because the sun that shines on the British shores is temperate and ". . . refines All things on which his radiance shines."[34] Jonson does not enact their actual epiphany; but when later we meet them in *Masque of Beauty*, their blackness has been washed away and they are throwing feasts of gratitude to Britannia, which has effected this transformation. The theme of Jonson's *Masque of Blackness*, the theme of blackness realizing its human ideal in whiteness, would thereafter be played out in Protestant churches in Africa where black converts sang with a fervor reminiscent of Jonson's twelve daughters of Niger: *"Wash me Redeemer and I shall be whiter than snow."* We find the postcolonial literary descendant of Jonson's daughters of Niger in Okot p'Bitek's *Song of Ocol*, where Ocol breaks down in a heart-wrenching cry:

> *Mother, mother*
> *Why*
> *Why was I born*
> *Black?*[35]

Unlike the fictional twelve daughters of Niger, Niger's actual sons and daughters could never have experienced physical epiphany; yet the view that blackness could be washed off by generous contact with Europe was carried out symbolically with the production of a European-languages-speaking elite and the attachment of European names to the body. A black character in my novel, *Wizard of the Crow,* suffers from white-ache, which can be cured only by his becoming white. Name and language loss are the necessary steps toward the loss of his previous identity and his renewal in the new identity. But his skin, alas, remains obstinately black, and he hires the services of a sorcerer who claims that he can bring about such color epiphany. African kids in French schools were forced to claim the Gauls as their ancestors, their African ones having been consigned to dark oblivion. An African character in Ousmane Sembene's film *Xala* explains to another why he cannot live in Spain: There are too many Negroes, he says. Fictional though they are, these creations certainly capture the essence of a class out of sync with its black being. The African elite's continued self-identification with Franco-, Anglo-, and Lusophonism attests to the burial of the Afro under layers of Europhonism.

V. Y. Mudimbe writes of colonialism as a confrontation of two types of societies, each with its own memory. A coherent colonial system, seemingly monolithic and supported by expansionist practices, faces "a multitude of African social formations with different and often particularist memories competing with each other," and binds them together. "Offering and imposing the desirability of its own memory, colonization promises a vision of progressive enrichment to the colonized."[36] He is describing the process by which the products of colonial educational factories may come to see the illusionary promises of the Europhone memory as the beginning of their history—a process that of course means the loss of their own history.

Brought up in that view of its land, its body, its history, this educated African elite was ultimately cut off from the social body by the ideology of self-abnegation. It began to see its own people as the enemy, a condition well captured in George Lamming's novel *In the Castle of My Skin*, set in Barbados and which depicts a native professional elite that in outlook acts like an overseer of colonial and, later, ex-colonial interests. The enemy is my people, writes Lamming of this group, in whom there develop suspicions, distrust, and even hostility toward its own people, whose uncivilized behavior the members of this elite see as letting their class down in the eyes of the white bourgeoisie. If only my people did not make demands, if only they spoke good English, if only they behaved, the group seems to be saying. But people do not speak and behave according to the standards of the colonizer. They make demands that cause the class of overseers to feel that the effectiveness of their role as overseers of their own people on behalf of the colonial authority is undermined. "You never can tell with my people. It was the language of the overseer, the language of the Government servant, and later the language of the lawyers and doctors who

had returned stamped like an envelope with what they called
the culture of the Mother Country."[37] Here Lamming is talking about the use of a particular common language, in this
case English, by an educated middle class, in this case Bar-
badian, to construct a self-serving class narrative that alien-
ates it from the people. The same kind of alienation, and
even attitudes, can occur with the choice of a language other
than the ones spoken by the people. The ambitious colonial
scheme of reconstructing an African whose historical, physical, and metaphysical geography begins with European
memory was almost realized with the production of such a native class dismembered from its social memory.

It is a double cultural decapitation: of a fraction of that
class dismembered from social memory through ideology
and of the class as a whole, dismembered through language.
For even where, in the continent, fractions of that class may
reject that European memory, they are dislodged from the social body by the languages of their education and storage of
knowledge.

Dismembered from the land, from labor, from power,
and from memory, the result is destruction of the base from
which people launch themselves into the world.

In war, all strategies and tactics revolve around the shield
and the spear. The defensive shield protects and consolidates
one's own base. The spear attacks, the goal being the capture
or destruction of the opponent's base, forcing him to retreat

and surrender. Applying the metaphor of war to systems of domination, we see that colonialism attacks and completely distorts a people's relationship to their natural, bodily, economic, political, and cultural base. And with this base destroyed, the wholeness of the African subject, the subject in active engagement with his environment, is fragmented.

It could be argued that the political and cultural struggles of Africans since the great dismemberment wrought by European slavery and then colonialism have been driven by the vision of wholeness. These struggles, taken as a whole, have been instrumental as strategies and tactics for remembering the fragmented. Indeed, they have comprised a quest for wholeness, the theme to which we turn in the next chapter.

CHAPTER TWO

RE-MEMBERING
VISIONS[1]

The oldest and best-known story of dismemberment and re-membering from African myth is the Egyptian story of Osiris, Isis, and Horus, the original trinity of father, mother, and only begotten son. It is a story that fascinates African writers: Ayi Kwei Armah of Ghana has published a novel, *Osiris Rising,* and Kamoji Wachira, while imprisoned by the postcolonial Kenya government for two years in a lonely camp where Mau Mau resistance fighters were tortured by the British in preindependence days, has written an epic in Gĩkũyũ, *Thagana Therera (River Thagana Flow),* addressed to Thagana, the main river in Kenya.[2] He finds himself evoking the inspirational memory of the Egyptian trinity in the Kenyan anticolonial resistance:

In the valley of your mother-in-law, the mighty Kiyiira,
Now nicknamed Nile, daughter of Namlolwe,
She too, like you, rolls and flows along, forever coursing
Towards the kingdom of Isis and Horus, the falcon
  god.
An old kingdom bequeathed them by their father
  Osiris,
He of the crown crested with twin plumes of white
  ostrich feather.
Kiyiira, Nile, who, like you, has suffered much
  triumph and pain,
She, understanding your cry of help, quickly
  answered you,
Took to heart the cause of your beloved folk—
  manacled and detained.
She thus inspired the whole world to cry shame to
  the British jailers of your fighters.
Thanks to her, Hola the death camp was closed.[3]

Kamoji Wachira is of course drawing parallels between the colonial and neocolonial tortures and hopes that the unity brought about by the river's circle of life will also cry shame to the neocolonial jailers.

Why does this Egyptian myth hold such fascination with writers in postcolonial Africa? Why does a political prisoner in solitary confinement in a semi-desert area in 1982 turn to a myth thousands of years old? According to Plutarch,[4] Osiris is killed by his evil brother, Set, who throws the coffin into the River Nile. Isis recovers the box and hides it. Set, who stumbles upon the recovered box, is angry and cuts Osiris's body into fourteen pieces, which he scatters all over Egypt. The indefatigable Isis, in an act of love and devotion, travels throughout Egypt and recovers the fragments, erecting a tomb to Osiris wherever she finds a piece. With the help of the deity Thoth, she re-members the fragments and restores Osiris to life. Out of the fragments and the observance of proper mourning rites comes the wholeness of a body re-membered with itself and with its spirit.

The fascination of these writers lies in the quest for wholeness, a quest that has underlain African struggles since the Atlantic slave trade. Though Ethiopianism and the like preceded these struggles, Garveyism and Pan-Africanism are the grandest secular visions for reconnecting the dismembered. Garveyism, with its Caribbean roots, unfolded on the terrain of America, but its vision—embodied in the title of Garvey's organization, the Universal Negro Improvement Association—was focused on the continent and its diaspora. "Africa for the Africans, those at home and those abroad" was the chorus of Garvey's speeches and plans. The name was meant to "embrace the purpose of all black humanity"[5]: to be free and equal members of the community of nations and peoples. For behind the rhetoric of blackness was also the universalist-humanist vision of using the Universal Negro Improvement Association to inspire African peoples "with pride in self and with the determination of going ahead in the creation of those ideals that will lift them to the unprejudiced company of races and nations. There is no desire for hate or malice, but every wish to see all mankind linked into a common fraternity of progress and achievement that will wipe away the odor of prejudice, and elevate the human race to the height of real godly love and satisfaction."[6] Garvey's detractors ignored this aspect of his thought. Re-membering the continent and the diaspora, the core theme of Pan-Africanism in general, was central to Garvey's vision of black people as active players in the world.

Dubois's Pan-Africanism, with its Afro-Caribbean, African-American, and continental African roots, saw the connection of the educated stratum to the masses as an absolute must in the fight to free African subjectivity—a fight best contained in the resolutions of the fifth Pan-African Congress held in Manchester in 1945. This Congress brought together African, Caribbean, and African-American intellectuals and political activists and came up with, among other resolutions, the now-famous Declaration to Colonial Peoples of the World, which placed African workers at the front line of the struggle against imperialism. The declaration called upon the intellectual and professional classes of the colonies to awaken to their responsibilities and join the workers in their fight for the right to form trade union and cooperatives, assemble freely, and hold demonstrations and strikes, and for the freedom to print and read literature, necessary for the education of the masses. "Today there is only one road to effective action—the organization of the masses. And in that organization, the educated must join."[7] What followed was an amazing historical turning point as the native political intellectuals returned to their domiciles in Africa, the Caribbean, and America to organize on the ground.

Garveyism and Pan-Africanism, as re-membering visions and practices, have had as their most visible results the gains of black civil rights in America, the independence of the Caribbean territories, the independence of Africa, and the rise of the Organization of African Unity (OAU) and, more recently, the African Union. Africa's role as the base of black history was always in Dubois's mind. "As I face Africa I ask myself: what is it between us that constitutes a tie which I can feel better than I can explain?"[8] he writes in *Dusk of Dawn*. In his life and works Dubois always explored the ties that bind, and within his oeuvre were several texts on Africa, including *The Negro* and *Africa and the World,* that defended Africa against racist accusations of nonachievement.[9]

In raising the issue of his inexplicable but still palpable ties to Africa, Dubois also forged an important link between the economic and political quest of African-Americans and those of Africans, which can be explained in terms of geographical origins, color, and a shared history of oppression with roots in slavery and colonialism. The psychological connections are not as easy to explain in empirical terms, but they can be felt in the souls of black folk. Dubois's book of the same title was a precursor to the Harlem Renaissance, which in turn inspired negritude. With its inspirational roots in the various Pan-Black movements such as Afro-Cubanism, Afro-Brazilianism, Haitian indigenism, and the Harlem Renaissance, and its current rebirth as Afro-centrism, negritude is the intellectual and literary reflection of Pan-Africanism. Garveyism centers on race; Pan-Africanism, on Africa and blackness; and negritude, on blackness. Afro-centrism, a method of viewing the world, is the opposite of Euro-centrism, which tends to see itself and the world around it as having a common original Greco-Roman center and the consequent conceptions, as Molefi Asante puts it, "of the foundation of civilization in a Greek miracle."[10]

In between the two cultural movements of negritude and Afro-centrism were the great assemblies of black writers— African, Afro-Caribbean, and African-American, first in Paris in 1956 and then in Rome in 1959. There was also the 1962

African writers' conference in Makerere, Uganda, which was at-
tended by, among others, Es'kia Mphahlele, Arthur Mamaine,
Bloke Modisane, Lewis Nkosi, Wole Soyinka, Chinua Achebe,
Christopher Okigbo, and J. P. Clark from South and West
Africa; Langston Hughes and Saunders Redding from America; and Arthur Drayton from the Caribbean. The Festac gatherings in Senegal in 1964 and Nigeria in 1976 drew an even
greater participation among black folk from around the world.

But whatever the differences in their emphasis, these
events were cultural and intellectual manifestations of the
quest for wholeness, and it is important that writers were at
the heart of such gatherings. Creative imagination is one of
the greatest of re-membering practices. The relationship of
writers to their social memory is central to their quest and
mission. Memory is the link between the past and the present, between space and time, and it is the base of our dreams.
Writers and the intellectuals in these movements are aware
that without a reconnection with African memory, there is no
wholeness. Not surprisingly, the theme of ancestor and past
is the most pronounced in negritude poetry—for instance, in
Léopold Senghor's prayer to masks "through whom the spirit
breathes"[11] or in his poem "Night of Sine," addressed to a
woman to whom he whispers a mix of endearments and sup-
plication to light the lamp of clear oil and "let the children in
bed talk about their ancestors, like their parents." His head on

her breast, he wants to "breathe the smell of our dead" and "contemplate and repeat their living voice."[12] This type of homage to the past became a necessary stage in the development of African writing—poetry, drama, and fiction. A good number of novelists also start with attempts at historical reconstruction. My own work, from *The River Between* through *Weep Not, Child* to *A Grain of Wheat*, forms a historical continuum from precolonial and colonial subjugation to anticolonial resistance to independence with a glance at the postindependence era. Frantz Fanon sees the claim to a national culture in the past as a dialectical negation of the perverted logic of colonialism, which "is not content to impose its rule upon the present and the future of a dominated country" nor "satisfied merely with holding a people in its grip and emptying the native's brain of all form and content," but "turns to the past of the oppressed people, and distorts, disfigures, and destroys it." Delving deep into their past, the colonial intellectuals found, to their joy, that the past was branded not with shame "but rather with dignity, glory and solemnity. Reclaiming the past . . . triggers a change of fundamental importance in the colonized's "psycho-affective equilibrium."[13]

Memory and consciousness are inseparable. But language is the means of memory, or, following Walter Benjamin, it is the medium of memory. It is here, in memory's very medium,

that the various movements' quest for wholeness seriously fal-
ters: Their relationship to both European and African languages remains problematic.

The problem of language and memory presents itself differently for the writers of the diaspora and of the continent.
In the diaspora, the question is this: How do you raise buried
memory from the grave when the means of raising it are
themselves buried in the grave or suffocated to the level of
whispering ghosts? And on the continent: Did the death intended for one's means of memory actually materialize? It is
my view that while the diasporic writer may in some way have
responded to the former question, those on the continent, at
least the visible majority, did not even argue about the question confronting them: that of the availability or effectiveness
of their native means of memory. Acting as if their native
means of memory were dead, or at least unavailable, the continental African chose to use the languages that buried theirs
so as to connect with their own memory—a choice that has
hobbled their re-membering literary visions and practices.
When reminded that African means of memory did not die,
some writers have reacted with indifference, hurt surprise, or
hostility, or have come up with arguments about the inade-
quacy of their own means of memory, or with cleverer claims
as to how borrowed means of memory can prove equally effective or even more effective in reconnection with their

memory—reactions not dissimilar to those of Anglophone writers in Ireland vis-à-vis Gaelic.

In an article that first appeared in the *New York Review of Books* some years ago, the Irish poet Nuala Ni Dhomhnaill talks of writing in Gaelic as a case of "the corpse that sits up and talks back."[14] She is referring to the fact that, even to her English writing contemporaries, Gaelic is assumed to be dead and the Anglophone-Irish tradition has taken on the mantle of the great tradition of Irish literature. In 1892, a hundred years before Dhomhnaill made these observations, and in response to nationalist calls for de-Anglicizing Ireland through the revival of Gaelic as championed by Douglas Hyde, Yeats could write to the editor of *United Ireland* that the "Gaelic language will soon be no more heard, except here and there in remote villages...."[15] He asks: "Can we not build a national tradition, a national literature, which shall be nonetheless Irish in spirit from being English in language? Can we not keep the continuity of the nation's life ... by translating or retelling in English, which shall have an indefinable Irish quality of rhythm and style, all that is best of ancient literature?"[16] English was to be used to make "a golden bridge between the old and the new."[17] The old was Gaelic; the new is English, of course. He compares the attempts to recall the Gaelic tongue to a longing for "the snows of yester-year."[18] At the same time, he insisted that efforts be made to prevent the decay of the Gaelic tongue; indeed, it should be preserved as "a learned language to be a fountain of nationality in our midst, but do not let us base upon it our hopes of nationhood."[19]

Yeats, who did not speak Gaelic but was nonetheless an important exponent of Irish nationalism, is a canonical figure in English studies in Africa, and his poetry has left a mark on African writing; his views on language may also have influenced African writers emerging from English departments. The Yeatsian attitude toward both English and Gaelic continues to this day, and the assumption in studies of Irish culture is that the English component speaks for all Irish literature. "By an antiquarian sleight of hand," writes Dhomhnaill, "it is implied that Irish writers in English are now the natural heirs to a millennium and a half of writing in Irish. The subtext of this . . . is that Irish is dead. . . . I dare say they must be taken somewhat aback when the corpse that they have long since consigned to choirs of angels . . . sits up and talks back."[20] The corpse talks back to announce that it is still alive—indeed, that it can speak for itself, and will not let the self-proclaimed heirs to its history cannibalize it with "equanimity, peddling their 'ethnic chic' with nice little translations 'From the Irish.'"[21]

This image, so apt in describing the relations between Gaelic and Anglophone-Irish, is equally applicable to the African linguistic situation. As we have seen, with linguicide occurring in the diaspora and linguifam on the continent, European memory sprouts on the graveyard of African memory. But African memory does not disappear quietly into that good night. It mounts resistance in both the African continent and the diaspora. However, given the linguistic fate of African languages in the two situations, the means of African memory in the diaspora and on the continent take different paths and hence face different questions.

Though his language may die, the diasporic African's memory of Africa does not itself turn into a corpse. It is nurtured in the field slave, who fashions his own means of keeping it alive. In time, out of the re-membered fragments of African speech and grammar the enslaved create new languages. They have different names in different places: Patois, Creole, Ebonics. Their orthographic representation is problematic, and they are often written as if they were misspelled English or French words. But they became languages, what Kamau Brathwaite calls "Nation languages," and they deserve adequate orthographies. In each case, these languages became the diasporic African's new means of survival, and the corpse, clothed in English-sounding words that are incomprehensible to the master at times, has now sat up and started talking back, telling stories, and singing. From the memory of African orature, what is often incorrectly characterized as oral literature, emerges African-American and Afro-Caribbean orature with trickster characters such as Hare and Anansi of the continent transformed into brother Rabbit and Anansi of the new world. The spirit begins to sing and out of it comes the great freedom spirituals whose force of beauty and imagery of hope and deliverance still make freedom sing everywhere in the world. The spiritual is an aesthetic of resistance, the most consistent and concentrated in world history. Out of that tradition of African-American and African-Caribbean speech, which produced the spiritual, came the blues, jazz, and calypso as well as today's reggae and hip-hop.

The corpse also began to write and, lo and behold, the Africa that slaves and their descendants were supposed to forget became the founding image of new visionary narratives. The image of Africa is there in every line of their poetry and prose. What is Africa to me?[22] asked the poet Countee Cullen in his poem "Heritage," and it is a question that many writers— from Phyllis Wheatley and Alice Walker to Toni Morrison and Kamau Brathwaite—have had to ask for themselves. Wheatley, the house girl, may remember Africa as a land of Egyptian gloom, but Oluado Equiano remembers it is as a land that is "uncommonly rich and fruitful, and produces all kinds of vegetables in great abundance,"[23] and, above all, as one of music and dance and poetry. "We are almost a nation of dancers, musicians, and poets,"[24] he writes in his narrative about himself. Jacques Roumain, in the poem "Guinea," addresses Africa directly: You are within me, he tells Africa, because he has kept her memory. As for Langston Hughes, the rivers he has known—rivers ancient as the world and older than the flow of blood in human veins, rivers that symbolize the depth, history, and self-renewal of his inheritance—include the Nile, the Congo, and the Mississippi. My soul, he proclaims, has grown deep like the rivers. At the height of the Caribbean renaissance of the 1950s was that famous exchange between V. S. Naipaul and George Lamming about the African presence in the Caribbean consciousness. Africa had been forgotten, proclaimed Naipaul, and films about African tribesmen were met with derisive West Indian laughter. It was precisely because Africa had not been forgotten, shot back Lamming, that West Indian embarrassment, in some, at least, took the form of derisive laughter, and he went on to cite the Calypso, which owes its character to the memory of Africa as "the basic folk rhythm of the Caribbean."[25]

The result of the diasporic African's interaction with his memory in a new environment is really astonishing when one contemplates what is really new in the Caribbean and modern American cultures. The new does not lie in the native cultures, for these were wiped out with the genocide of the Caribs, or imprisoned in the reservations as in the case of Native Americans. The achievements of Native Americans, despite the decimation of their cultures, are not in doubt—but then, the Native American still resides in his homeland. Writers like Simon Ortiz are aware of their heritage: They can even point to the sacred grounds of their ancestors.

Nor does the new reside in the Euro-Caribbean and Euro-American; for, whether in language, poetry, or architecture, the Euro-American sees himself as a continuation of the European inheritance. Whatever innovations he may bring into his creation, and there is no doubt about the achievements of the Euro-American genius, he does so within his inherited European tradition. He begins with imitation long before he starts to innovate. One need only look at the architecture of Yale and Harvard, which clearly imitated that of Oxford and Cambridge, utilizing stones specially treated to make them look old. Indeed, when Cambridge is discussed, the listener often does not know which Cambridge one is talking about—the British Cambridge or the American Cambridge—unless a qualification is added for clarity. The Euro-American is conscious of a history of which he is an heir, and this history is that of Europe. T. S. Eliot, Ezra Pound, Henry James, Gertrude Stein, and Ernest Hemingway all returned to Europe to drink from the source of their culture. They were able to return because their link to the European linguistic base had never been ruptured. For a long time, Euro-American literature remained beholden to the older culture. Even in terms of academic organization, it is the English department, not the American literature department, that is still the centerpiece of the humanities and liberal arts in the American academy.

The African-American tells a different story. Cut off from continuous contact with Africa, and yet thrust into the center of modern capitalist production—C.L.R. James calls the New Africans the modern proletariat[26]—they had to innovate or perish. Even the corpse into which their languages had been turned metamorphosed into a spirit haunting European languages, English mostly. Black speech infuses the supposedly Euro-American official mainstream. That is why Zora Neale Hurston could rightfully assert in "Characteristics of Negro Expression" that "the American Negro has done wonders to the English language.... [H]e has made over a great part of the tongue to his liking and has [had] his revision accepted by the ruling class. No one listening to a Southern white man talk could deny this. Not only has he softened and toned down strongly consonanted words like 'aren't' to 'ain't' and the like, he has made new force words out of old feeble elements."[27] Black speech is as integral to Mark Twain as it is to William Faulkner, for instance, and of course black music is central to the American mainstream. Grabbing, clutching whatever lay around them and washing it in the ancient rivers of the African memory that would not die, diasporic Africans created the truly original in music, dance, song, and prose in American and Caribbean cultures—a feat whose triumph, despite the turbulence of history, is celebrated in the poetry of Kamau Brathwaite.

> *For on this ground*
> *trampled with the bull's swathe of whips*
> *where the slave at the crossroads was a red anthill*

eaten by moonbeams, by holy ghosts
of his wounds
the Word becomes
again a god and walks amongs us;
look, here are his rags,
here is his crutch and his satchel
of dreams; here is his hoe and his rude implements
on this ground
on this broken ground[28]

At the end of *The Arrivants*, a new-world trilogy that includes *Rights of Passage, Islands,* and *Masks,* Kamau Brathwaite concludes with the vision of those among whom the god walks, on that broken ground:

now waking
making
with their
rhythms some-
thing torn
and new.[29]

What about the continent? Here African languages may have been shut out of the classroom, marketplace, and administration. They may indeed have been forced to whisper like hungry ghosts. But they did not die; they were kept alive by the peasantry in the culture of the everyday and in the great tradition of orature. Like their counterparts in the field slaves, the peasantry as a whole, speaking Yoruba, Wolof, Akan, and Zulu—and the whole lot of languages in Africa— remain the collective griot, the keepers of communal memory. They do whatever they can to express the world in their own languages, sometimes even absorbing words from the English or French or other tongues, as all living languages tend to do.

One cannot say the same of dwellers in the European masters' linguistic mansion. They are the elite cut off from the social body. Sent by the community to get knowledge from the wider world, they rarely return, and when they do, it is as strangers. In *Arrow of God*,[30] Chinua Achebe tells the story of Oduche, who is sent to the new school by Ezeulu, the chief priest of his own people, with a specific mission to find out what is there and, if it is good, to bring him his share. However, Oduche learns enough to make him feel sufficiently bold to come back home and imprison a sacred python. He would have killed it but, instead, traps it in a box. Oduche's story is that of all other graduates of the prison-house of European languages. He captures the python, the symbol of his people's being, and imprisons it in a box to suffocate and possibly die. I always remember how, upon learning how to read in English, my classmates and I would carry the English-language bible to church. The service was entirely in Gĩkũyũ. Everybody else had the Gĩkũyũ-language bible. The preacher read passages from the Gĩkũyũ-language bible. But we who had been to school would follow him through our English text. The Gĩkũyũ voice had to come to us in English sounds.

This was to become the practice in African writing as well. Almost as if borrowing from the Yeatsian text, African writers cannibalized African lives and African memory. What they created, even when it is the masterpiece of a ventriloquist, is locked up in Oduche's box, accessible to the owners of the language and those of the writer's folk who have the linguistic key. Like the Anglo-Irish literature that took the mantle of Irish literature, Europhone-African literature has stolen the identity of African literature. The case of Ireland is different in the sense that English had become the majority language spoken, as the mother tongue, even by those who advocated the Gaelic revival. In that sense the Irish case is closer to that of the African diaspora, where English, or some forms of it, became willy-nilly the majority language of the diaspora, a kind of foster-mother tongue. But on the continent the majority still speak African languages. Growing up in two different contexts since the great dismemberment, the diasporic and educated continental Africans came to have two different attitudes toward African memory and means of memory.

We can see this even in the conception of negritude in the diaspora versus negritude on the continent. Negritude was born of the interactions between diasporic and continental Africans in the streets and classrooms of Paris in between the wars, symbolized by the trio of Sedar Senghor from Senegal, Aimé Césaire from Martinique, and Leon Damas from Guinea. These three conceived it as they collaborated on the periodical *L'Etudiant Noir*. But though certain common themes and imagery run through their poetry and Césaire specifically acknowledges the role of Senghor in making him aware of Africa and its singularity, their brands of negritude have different implications, almost contradictory with respect to African memory. In a 1967 interview with the Haitian poet René Depestre reproduced in Césaire's *Discourse on Colonialism,* Césaire says that his discovery of his negritude in between the wars proceeded from his realization that though he was French and bore the marks of French customs, and had been branded by Cartesian philosophy and French rhetoric, if he broke with all that and plumbed the depths of his unconscious, what he would find was fundamentally black. It was a plunge into Africa for me, he says, adding: "... I felt that beneath the social being would be found a profound being, over whom all sorts of ancestral layers and alluviums had been deposited."[31] His plunge into Africa was a way of emancipating his consciousness. Césaire did not have an African language.

But he plunged into what African languages had produced in his strife "to create a new language, one capable of communicating the African heritage . . . an Antellean French, a black French that, while still being French, had a black character."[32] There is a Yeatsian ring to this declaration.

But Senghor—unlike Césaire, for whom French was his mother tongue—had an African language. He came from an African-language community. His plumbing the depths of Africa had a necessarily different purpose: He cannibalized what African languages had produced so as to enrich the French language. His famous statement that emotion was to Africa what logic was to the Greeks—and the necessity of their synthesis as expressed in so many of his poems in the image of the blood that the Western civilization needed to oil its rusty joints—put him in the position of Oduche: seeking to imprison the African python in a French box. Whereas Césaire's position is closer to that of Yeats, who wanted to plunge into the Irish heritage to create from it an Anglophone-Irish literature that had an Irish character, Senghor's position is closer to that of Matthew Arnold in relation to Welsh and the Celtic heritage. For him, Celtism was a depository of a spiritual power from which the Saxons could draw. And it is as an archeological site of sentiment and spiritual power that Matthew Arnold advocated its study in his four lectures as chair of poetry at Oxford. Otherwise, for purposes of entry into modernity, "the sooner the Welsh language disappears as an instrument of the practical, political, social life of Wales, the better; the better for England, the better for Wales itself."[33] A Welsh writer could use Welsh to say something about punctuality, "but the moment he has anything of real importance to say, anything the world will the least care to hear, he must speak English.... For all modern purposes ... let the Welshman speak English, and, if he is an author, let him write English."[34] But Arnold waxes almost lyrical in the defense of the Celtic genius of Welsh as a has-been, a relic, useful only as a source of spiritual vitality for Saxon English. Apart from its counting for "a good deal, far more than we Saxons, most of us, imagine, as a spiritual power," such Welsh could be a useful subject for the science of origins and for comparative philology.[35] Here Arnold combines, on the one hand, the Yeatsian enthusiasm for an innate "wild Celtic blood, the most un-English of all things under heaven"[36] from which to create an Anglophone literature to express Irish modernity and, on the other, sixteenth-century Spenserian sentiments vis-à-vis Gaelic, whose virtue lay in its being a dead language, useful only for study as antiquity.

The Celtism that Arnold talks about and the Yeatsian "wild Celtic blood" are very close to Senghorian negritude, a vital force that could be extracted to add ethnic chic to his contribution to French as the language of universal civiliza-tion. Senghor hardly ever talked of enriching any African language, and the only time he showed enthusiasm for African languages was when he banned Ousmane Sembene's *Ceddo* (a brilliant film about slavery in which the characters actually speak their own language) because Sembene had spelled Ceddo with two d's instead of one. It is not surpris-ing that Senghor—one of the high priests of negritude, who always kept his French citizenship, even as the head of state of an independent African country—ended up as guardian of the sacred academy that oversees the growth of French, an in-stitution founded in 1635 by Cardinal Richelieu. Senghor's case may be a little extreme, but it is essentially not different from that of the postcolonial African middle class as a whole, of whom it can be said (as Nuala Ni Dhomhnaill did with re-spect to the Anglophone-Irish) that "far be it from them to make the real effort to learn the living language[s],"[37] because, I might add, they prefer them dead.

How does one begin to explain this attitude of the African bourgeoisie toward the languages of their cultures? It is not enough to say that European languages were imposed, though true, because African languages, while famished and shut out of power, never really suffered linguicide. Perhaps one can explain such an attitude in terms of Frantz Fanon's characterization of this class as having an almost incurable

desire for the permanent identification with its Western elders, "from whom it has learnt its lessons."[38] Even this, though
true, does not quite explain why the middle class in Africa
wholly sees itself and identifies itself as European-language
speaking. For one would think that the need to urge the nation toward higher resolves in such areas as economic enterprise, health management, political engagement, and
cultural imagination would lead the middle class to resort to
the only re-membering practice capable of moving the nation
forward—that of connecting to the languages the actors in
the social drama of change actually speak. Nevertheless, the
middle class prefers the European linguistic screen that keeps
it worlds apart from the people. In all other societies, writers,
keepers of memories, and carriers of national discourse use
the languages of their communities; but the postcolonial intellectuals prefer to express communal memories in foreign
languages, which, in the end, means sharing those communal
memories with the foreign owners of the languages or among
themselves as a foreign-language-speaking elite. The result,
really, is an intra-class conversation of an elite that, cocooned
from the people by the language of its choice and practice,
conceives of itself as constituting the nation all by itself. The
Arnoldian and Yeatsian enthusiasm for the Celtic languages
as exquisite corpses, archeological mines for helping create an
English ringing with rhythms different from those of the

original owner's standard English, yet still recognizably English—this is the model of the African intelligentsia.

We may have to borrow from psychoanalysis to explain the formerly colonized natives' death wish for the languages of their cultures. The trauma of death is often overcome by mourning, whether individually or as a collective experience of grief. To mourn is to acknowledge the loss, to purge oneself of the negative effects of trauma. In African societies, mourning, always a collective rite, can go on for days, as Ghanaian scholar-musicologist J. H. Nketia attests in his classic study of this phenomenon, *Funeral Dirges of the Akan People:* "The celebration of a funeral is regarded as a duty and no pains are spared to make it a memorable event."[39] The celebration consists of five phases of preparation for the funeral: pre-burial mourning including the wake, internment, after-burial mourning, and subsequent periodic mourning. Underlying the importance of mourning is the African worldview of the unity of the dead, the living, and the unborn. "There are beliefs in the visitations of the dead, in invisible participation of the dead in the life of this world and the continuation of ties of kithship and kinship after death. Consequently, the living are anxious to keep up good relations with the dead, to remember them, to show concern for them, to identify themselves with them and to ask their favour."[40] Mourning, then, is a somber celebration of a rite of passage in the journey of the trinity, but it is also a memory, a re-membering of the ancestors, an honoring of the heritage they have left to the living. It is a closure and an opening to a new relationship of being.

What are the consequences of a lack of mourning? Nicolas Abraham and Maria Torok talk of situations in which individuals suffering a trauma do not mourn and come to a closure. They shut the trauma in a psychic tomb, acting as if the loss never happened. The radical denial of loss means no mourning at all, for you cannot mourn a loss you deny. "The words that cannot be uttered, the scenes that cannot be recalled, the tears that cannot be shed—everything will be swallowed along with the trauma that led to the loss."[41] A mourning that cannot be expressed "erects a secret tomb inside the subject,"[42] what Abraham and Torok call a crypt; "psychic tombs meant to stay sealed off from self, interior tombs for the ghosts of the past," as Gabriele Schwab puts it.[43] The denial of loss and, hence, the lack of mourning can occur at the group level; kept in a collective crypt, the trauma can be passed on transgenerationally as "the unfinished business of a previous generation"[44] to haunt the future. Extending Abraham and Torok's explanation to include certain silences in post-Nazi Germany and drawing on her own experience of growing up in the post-Nazi era, Schwab demonstrates how "untold or unspeakable, unfelt or denied pain, concealed shame, covered-up crimes or violent histories continue to affect and disrupt the lives of those involved in them."[45] Such crypts engender silence, she adds, such as the one she witnessed among her elders in their avoidance of references to what had already happened. She is talking of the transgenerational trauma experienced by the children of perpetrators of horror against others, but her observation is equally applicable to the children of the recipients of horror.

Postcolonial Africa has never properly mourned the deaths that occurred in the two traumatic events in its history: slavery and colonialism. Many thousands died on land and in the sea. Others perished on slave plantations in the world of their captivity and in colonial plantations such as the rubber plantations of Belgian Congo and the gold and diamond mines of South Africa. Millions more died in the fights against slave trade, slavery, and colonialism. Altogether, it was an African holocaust, or horrordom. Those who fell never had a proper burial, nor were they periodically mourned in the way that Nketia talks about. Kenya, which regained its independence from more than sixty years of British colonial rule, is a good example of this denial. In place of re-membering, there was a systematic attempt to act as if Kenya's independence had come as a gift from the Queen of England, very much as the liberation of slaves was often touted as a gift from the good Queen Victoria. Liberation, being a gift honoring the fallen, was not going to be part of the postcolonial memory.

Upon independence, some playwrights wanted to stage a play to celebrate the struggles and remember those who died in the mountains and concentration camps of the British colonial state. They wanted the spirits of the fallen to be with Kenyans at the moment of hoisting the flag of our independence, the result of years of bloodshed. But the government stopped the play; one minister stated that this was not the way Kenya would be embarking on its independence. In his book *Race Against Time,* British writer Richard Frost, a diplomat at the time that Kenya attained its independence, narrates this incident with approval.

This is what the Kenyan poet Kamoji Wachira decries in his epic poem *Thagana Therera,* in which he attributes the rot of postcolonial Kenya society to that neglect of the dead, as if the lamentations of those who never received proper mourning still haunt the country's independence. That is why he begs the river to awaken the memory of the living to the crime committed by the Kenyan nation in not mourning the thousands who fell in their fight against the British colonial state—men and women who shed their blood that we might live as free men and women.

> *Why do these monstrous curses rain upon us?*
> *Were some first-borns' after-birth left to wild beasts?*
> *Is there an unpaid debt the founder and his*
>   *progeny left to our ancestors—*

A debt never settled or blessed with the right
   ceremonies? ...
Maybe charms left unburied, or weapons of defeat
   re-used without cleansing?
Oh yes, perhaps the stale tears left too long unshed,
   festering inside
For those countless dead never yet mourned
Killed at war defending your lands, mighty
   river....[46]

The unity of the dead, the living, and the unborn is broken. There is no healing, no wholeness; only a dislocation of the national psyche, for in not remembering the past, there are no inherited ideals by which to measure the excesses of the present. Kenya is not alone in this.

In the continent as a whole, the postcolonial slumber would not be disturbed by memories of the African holocaust. Slavery and colonialism become events of shame, of guilt. Their memory is shut up in a crypt, a collective psychic tomb, which is what Oduche symbolically does when he shuts the python, a central image of his people's cosmic view, in a box. Abraham and Torok say that a people's shutting of unwanted memories in a crypt can lead to a kind of hiding in language, what they call "cryptonymy."[47] And Nketia points to an intimate bond between mourning and language when he observes that "the requirements of social life often impose forms of linguistic behaviour on individuals or groups of individuals in given situations, to which are attached values that appear to govern their continued practice. The study of verbal expressions in such situations is important not only for a clearer understanding of the problems of meaning in a language, but also for a deeper understanding of a people's life from which their meaning is ultimately derived. In Akan social life, one such situation is the funeral."[48] Cryptonymy as developed by Abraham and Torok refers to "operations in language that emerge as manifestations of a psychic crypt, often in the form of fragments, distortions, gaps and ellipses."[49] Abraham and Torok are talking of lapses and ellipses that occur in a single language. But cryptonymy can also take the form of hiding in another language altogether. Immigrants into new societies, especially those who are escaping their own histories, have been known to consciously and deliberately refuse to teach their children their own language, the language of the country and history from which they are in flight, so as to facilitate their assimilation into the country and culture of adoption. Erasure of memory is the condition of such assimilation—whether forced, induced, or willing— and the new language becomes a screen against the past that they do not want their children to face.

The cryptonic practices of an African bourgeoisie that never properly acknowledged the traumatic reality of slave trade and colonial tortures likewise take the form of hiding in

European languages, erecting a barrier to a deeper understanding of their history and distancing them from their history as felt experience. Within the crypt the writer experiences
double pleasure: He has screened himself from the trauma,
the shame of defeat, the shame of a language or culture of defeat; and yet, at the same time, he freely borrows from the language of shame to claim a separate identity in the language of
victory. He imagines that the death of the language of shame
allows him to create freely in the language of victory and
earn a place in the universality of European languages. This
death wish for African languages by African intellectuals and
states is reminiscent of Ben Jonson's daughters of Niger trav-
eling to the English shores to be washed white. The African
son and daughter of Niger are symbolically washed white by
language. From their Europhonic standpoint, they can now
look at their former language as outsiders looking in, and can
even contemplate it, à la Spenser and Arnold, as a "has-been,"
a subject of philological enquiry, an antiquity from which they
can occasionally borrow a proverb or two to spice their mas-
tery of the English.

Here then is the major difference between the continental African and the diasporic African. Forced into a crypt, the
African in the diaspora tries to break out of the crypt, and
grasps whatever African memory he can reach, to invent a
new reality. On the continent, the reformed African tries to
enter the crypt and store his inventions there.

It seems to me that what is needed is to break out of the crypt. We have to confront the realities of our past and mourn the dead in the proper way. Zora Neale Hurston must have had such an idea in mind when in 1945 she proposed to W.E.B. Dubois the purchase of a hundred acres for "a cemetery for the illustrious Negro dead," so that "no Negro celebrity, no matter what financial condition they might be in at death, lie in inconspicuous forgetfulness. We must assume the responsibility of their graves being known and honored." The lack of such "a tangible thing allows our people to forget, and their spirits evaporate."[50] But this should obviously be more than a single physical site for the remembrance of a few. It is a matter of re-membering the entirety of Pan-Africa. Every year across the continent and the entire diaspora there should be a month, a week, even just a day of collective mourning for the millions whose souls still cry for proper burial and accordance of proper mourning rites. And accompanying these formal performances should be works of art, music, literature, dance, and cinema that connect our past to our present as a basis for the future. But one cannot honor the dead, engage the living, or create dreams of tomorrow in foreign voices: Those rites can be wrought only in the languages of the loved ones. "Is it enough," asks the Ghanaian poet Kofi Anyidoho, "to dream in foreign languages and drink champagne in banquet halls of a proud people while our people crack palm kernels with their teeth?"[51] It is not enough, it is not enough, he answers, thus linking the question of language to that of material being. Let the caged bird sing, but let it sing in its own language.

If history is replete with the death of languages as a result of the physical or cultural death of the peoples who spoke them, there have also been cases where languages have been resurrected from the dead to walk among the living and express the life of the living: Israel, for instance, needed the resurrection of Hebrew to reconnect with the ancient memory it carried; the resurrected became the means of new memories. Continental Africa is in a unique position because African languages have not yet died. But they are not part of the expression of national life, or, rather, are only an expression of the peasant; however, in that position, they remain invisible, literary-wise, buried alive under the weight of European languages—ironically, in much the same way that European languages used to be in the Middle Ages, invisible under the weight of Latin, before they found new life during the Renaissance. This is the theme of the next chapter.

CHAPTER THREE

MEMORY, RESTORATION, AND AFRICAN RENAISSANCE[1]

In recent years, there has been much talk, in addition to a spate of books, about an African renaissance. Responding to these currents, Manthia Diawara in 1994 launched the journal *Black Renaissance/Renaissance Noir*. But even before this, throughout the twentieth century, the word *renaissance* repeatedly cropped up in reference to the South African Xhosa and Zulu writers of the early twentieth century—Samuel Edward Krune Mqhayi and Benedict W. Vilikazi as well as the Dhlomo brothers, H.I.E. Dhlomo and R.R.R. Dhlomo, among them. In 1948 Cheikh Anta Diop used the term when he posed the conditions necessary for an African renaissance. And of course there was the Harlem Renaissance, the surge of black writing that included such luminaries as Langston Hughes, Zora Neale Hurston, Claude Mackay, and Countee Cullen.

Renaissance describes a moment when the quantity and quality of intellectual and artistic output are perceived as signaling "a monumental historical shift"[2] in the life of a people, nation, or region. This phenomenon is not peculiar to Africa; indeed, there has been much talk of other renaissances in different histories and cultures. A book appropriately titled *Other Renaissances* contains chapters on Arab, Bengali, Tamil, Chinese, Harlem, Mexican, Maori, Chicago, Hebrew, and Irish renaissances;[3] ironically, however, it makes no mention of any African renaissances, despite recent discussion of a Sophiatown renaissance as well as of African renaissance in general.

But any talk of renaissance invites a comparison with the European Renaissance, a term coined in the nineteenth century to refer to the Europe of the fourteenth through sixteenth centuries.[4] This era occurred between the Middle Ages and the Enlightenment, coinciding with the beginnings of capitalist modernity. Such a comparison is inevitable for Africa because European capitalist modernity, emerging out of those voyages of the body and mind, was rooted in slave trade, slavery, and colonialism. Marx cites the turning of Africa into a warren for the hunting of black skins alongside the entombment of the original inhabitants in the gold and silver mines of America as signaling the rosy dawn of capitalism, a capitalism that came dripping with blood and dirt to the core. This act literally turned Africa into the dark side of the European Enlightenment, a darkness that lasted from the seventeenth century to the mid-twentieth century. What ensued was a hiatus in African development—that is, development seen as organically arising out of a balanced interplay of the internal and external contradictions in society. It put in motion what Walter Rodney has described as the development of underdevelopment.[5]

The hiatus may be described as an African middle ages, encompassing the entire slave and colonial period, during which Africa was dismembered from its past. When European writers referred to Africa as the Dark Continent or wrote novels on themes of darkness, they were ironically referring to what they had created with their kind of light. It was quite insightful of Conrad to see the gates to the *Heart of Darkness* of his novel as lying in European warehouses. Thames and Brussels were the gates into the heart of darkness where people were hunted down on account of their color and the shape of their nose.

There are significant parallels between the African and European middle ages. The European Renaissance marked the end of the European Dark Ages; the same Renaissance marked the beginnings of the African dark ages. If the picture of the world during the European dark ages was centered in God, Church, and universal empire, that of Africa was centered in a white God, Mother-country, and colonial empires. Can we meaningfully compare the African and European renaissances? The tendency in the current discussion of an African renaissance is to refer to it as a desirable ideal, an outcome that can be willed into being rather than a thing that has already happened or is happening now. To a certain extent this is true: A full-fledged renaissance has yet to flower.

Nevertheless, the African renaissance has already started: It began at the historical moment when the idea of Africa became an organizing force in opposition to the European colonial empires. V. Y. Mudimbe describes the idea of Africa as a product of the West's system of self-representation, which included creation of an otherness conceived and conveyed through conflicting systems of knowledge.[6] But I prefer to think of the idea of Africa—or, more appropriately, the "African idea," as African self-representation. To distinguish it from the Mudimbeist formula according to which Europe is finding itself through its invention of Africa, I see the African idea as that which was forged in the diaspora and traveled back to the continent.

In the diaspora, Africans could see the whole continent as the home they were forced to leave no matter how they viewed their exile—as mercy in the case of Phyllis Wheatley, or as tragic loss in the case of Equiano and those who sang of feeling like motherless children a long way from home. The African idea in the diaspora finds its most dramatic self-realization in the independence of Haiti in the eighteenth century. In recognition of the centrality of Haiti in the African idea, C.L.R. James's *The Black Jacobins*, published in 1938, and written with Africa in mind, suggested that what the Haitians had done to counter plantation slavery—defeating the combined efforts of the most advanced Europeans of the day, including the expedition to restore slavery led by Napoleon's own brother—could be replicated in Africa and the entire Caribbean region in the twentieth century. Aimé Césaire describes Haiti as the place where negritude was born. In this context the African idea was not simply a reaction to Europe's self-representation with Africa as its otherness but a consciousness in organized opposition to the oppressing otherness that was Europe. It was this African idea that put in motion the rebirth of Africa. The European Renaissance was coterminous with the emergence of modern Europe from the Dark Ages of a tottering feudalism and a Catholic papacy; the African renaissance is coterminous with an emerging Afro-modernity from the dying colonialism of European empires. The European Renaissance launched European modernity; the African renaissance evolving in the struggle against the dark side of European modernity gave birth to Afro-modernity.

There are other important markers in the evolution of Afro-modernity (the 1900 Pan-African congress in London, for instance, or the 1914 birth of Garvey's Universal Negro Improvement Association in Jamaica); but the formation of the African National Congress (ANC) in 1912 on the continent crystallized the African idea as an active agency in the constitution of the Afro-modern. The ANC was the first modern political organization on the continent to bring Africans of different cultural ethnicities together to fight for their place in the sun—or a place on which to lay their burden, to use the Garveysian phrase. This momentous event was inspired by the ideas of the New Negro Movement and Pan-Africanism in America, where some of the ANC's founders had interacted with the thoughts of Alexander Crummwell, Booker T. Washington, Marcus Garvey, and W.E.B. Dubois.[7] Pixley Ka Isaka Seme, one of the founders of the ANC, and who in 1904 had written an essay titled "The Regeneration of Africa," studied at Jesus College in Oxford and at Columbia University in America. He was friends with Alain Locke, editor of *The New Negro*. In the years from 1896 to 1900, Charlotte Manya Maxeke—another founder member and, later, president of its women's league—was a student of W.E.B. Dubois at Wilberforce University, where she became friends with Nina Gomer, Dubois's wife. Solomon T. Plaaje interacted with Dubois in the early 1920s in Harlem.[8]

The ANC was predicated on the African idea. Its anthem, *Nkosi Sikelele Afrika*, took the entire continent as the theater of its appeal and vision. Its creation marked Africans' awakening to practical necessity and their ability to confront European capitalist modernity in its white colonial robes. Whatever the regional modifications and specificities, all other modern political parties in the continent followed the tracks of the ANC—some, including the Malawi National Congress, the Rhodesia National Congress, Uganda People's Congress, incorporating part of its name. Others, such as Kwame Nkrumah's Convention People's Party (CPP), the Zimbabwe African National Union (Zanu), the Zimbabwe African People's Union, and the Kenya African National People's Union (Kanu), embodied the idea of a congress of African peoples transcending ethnicities.

If we were to turn around the Hegelian contention that history as the embodiment of reason, which in turn is the embodiment of freedom, started in the East and found its apotheosis in the West, we can say that the African idea as the quest for freedom on a Pan-African scale extended from the diaspora to the continent and back again. It is a dialectical play of the ties that bind, to borrow a notion from W.E.B. Dubois's *Dusk of Dawn*, in the fight to break out of the dark mantle of night with which Europe had wrapped Africa. Dubois's mantra of colorful lights with which he sings of Africa opposes Hegel's mantle of the night with which he wraps Africa.

The African idea became the animating force of modern politics in the continent; for whether in Kenya, Nigeria, Angola, or Senegal, people viewed themselves as Africans. This is not to say that continental Africans began to struggle against European occupation in the beginning of the twentieth century but, rather, that they had previously fought back as Zulus (in the Zulu wars); as IsiXhosa (in the Xhosa wars); and as Ashanti, Gīkūyū, or Ibo. The qualitative difference was their self-perception as Africans: They organized themselves under modern political parties as Africans. Zik (Nnamdi Azikiwe), who spearheaded the Nigerian struggle, titled his book *Resurgent Africa;* Kwame Nkrumah titled his *Towards African Freedom.* And just as the emergence of the modern in Europe was being reflected in the efflorescence of the arts, preceding it, surrounding it, and emanating from it, the 1912 moment was preceded, surrounded, then followed by a spate of important writings in South Africa, mainly in African languages[9]—although there was contention over whether English or the African languages were the best means of Afromodernity's self-realization. Examples of works written in African languages include S.E.K. Mqhayi's poetry in *Izwi la Bantu, 1892–1900* and his novella, *Ityla Lamwele* (1914); Walter Benson's *Zemki Imkomo Magwilandimi* (1906); and Magema Frize's *Abantu Abammnyama* (1922).

But the real turning point in the drama of Afro-modernity was the 1945 Manchester Congress, which, among other things, called upon the intellectuals and professional classes of the colonies to awaken to their responsibilities and join the masses to oust colonial rule.[10] This effort resulted in the "*Dec-*

laration to Colonial Peoples of the World," to which leaders like Kwame Nkrumah and Jomo Kenyatta responded by returning to Africa from their domiciles abroad to lead the continent out of the dark ages of colonial empire and into an era of African enlightenment. What resulted were the remarkable decades of the 1950s and 1960s, whose drama and pace of change were completely unprecedented in world history. Country after country in Africa reclaimed their independence, announcing themselves as players on the modern stage—and, in the process, reshaping that stage, or at least the color of it. Each country may have emerged as a nation-state, territorially speaking, but beneath their national colors all of their peoples saw themselves as Africans. The journey of the African idea, beginning in Haiti and championed by Pan-African congresses, reached its climax in the independence of Angola, Guinea Bissau, and Mozambique and the liberation of South Africa in the 1980s and 1990s.

The independence of African countries ushered in true Afro-modernity. The launching of the ANC in 1912 and its accession to power in 1994 framed a crucial century that witnessed the beginnings of the African renaissance and the drama of the Afro-modernity of which it is a part. These decades saw explosions in the arts—music, dance, and the plastic arts—as well as in African writing in European languages, a trend that continues to the present. Thus, just as the energy, vigor, and impetus of the European renaissance in the

arts were only expressions, at the aesthetic level, of the energy
and heat generated by the tensions and contradictions in
the meeting point of two epochs—the old and the new, a dying world and another struggling to be born—much the
same was true of Africa where the vigor, contradictions, and
tensions of decolonization were transmitted in the arts and
aesthetic vibrations of the new age. To the question

> *Africa tell me Africa*
> *Is this you this back that is bent*
> *This back breaking under the weight of humiliation*
> *This back trembling with red scars*
> *And saying yes to the whip under the midday sun*

a grave but clearly optimistic voice could answer:

> *That tree there*
> *In splendid loveliness amidst white and faded flowers*
> *That is Africa your Africa*
> *That grows again patiently obstinately*
> *And in its fruit gradually acquires*
> *The bitter taste of liberty.*[11]

Artists do not create the tensions and conflicts in society; they
respond to them, giving them shape, form, and direction or

perhaps just recording them—and this is as true of the African artists of the twentieth and twenty-first centuries as it is of the European Renaissance artists centuries earlier. And much like the European Renaissance, which began in fourteenth-century Italy and on the rest of the Western seaboard during the sixteenth century, the African renaissance has not been uniform or drastic: It has blossomed earlier in some places, later in others. And again, just as the European Renaissance begat the nation-states of Italy, Portugal, Spain, France, and England, the African renaissance has borne many nation-states of its own.

Even the contradictions of the ages are comparable. Those in the midst of the European Renaissance could view it as an expression of both hope and hopelessness. Erasmus of Rotterdam, for instance, alternated between denouncing it as corruption ("When was there ever more tyranny? When did avarice reign more largely and less punished?") and lauding it as the "near approach of a golden age," the dawn of a new world, making him wish he could grow young again; and even then he went back to denouncing it as the "irremediable confusion of everything."[12] It was an age of massacres, most prominent of which was the Saint Bartholomew Massacre in Paris in 1572. It was an age of wars between and within the new nation-states, such as the conflicts involving England and Spain or the Thirty Years' War in Germany between 1618 and

1648. In the same way one could see, in what has been un-
folding in Africa, the faces of Nyerere, Mandela, Kofi Annan,
Soyinka, Mafouz, Bishop Tutu, and Wangari Maathai, or
those of Moi, Mobutu, Idi Amin, or Bokassa—the faces of rising democracies or reigning military dictatorships. The
avarice, tyranny, and confusion that appalled Erasmus of
Rotterdam apply also to postcolonial Africa, where diseases,
famines, and massacres beset places like Rwanda, Darfur,
Liberia, and Sierra Leone. Hope and hopelessness still con-
tend for domination of the African soul as they did for that of
the European soul.

But there the similarities end. The European Renaissance
lasted three centuries (four if we include the thirteenth and
five if we include the seventeenth), whereas the African renaissance is just a century old. The European Renaissance is
a thing of the past, and we know the kind of modernity it generated and understand its impact on the world; the African
renaissance is a work in progress, and we cannot predict its
ultimate shape, destiny, or impact on Afro-modernity and the
world.

The European intellectual movement was a reflection—
in terms of ideas, ethics, and aesthetics—of fundamental
changes in the organization of the production of wealth within
the womb of the feudal societies of Europe. A blooming mercantile capitalism, Marx wrote, "gave to commerce, to navigation, to industry an impulse never before known, and

thereby, to the revolutionary element in the tottering feudal society, a rapid development."[13] This "revolutionary element" was the rising middle class, which sought and needed freedom from the ecclesiastical laws, the closed guilds, and a view of the world that denied it movement.

It is true that the African middle class, which led the faction committed to anticolonial nationalism, wanted freedom from colonial laws, racial barriers, and a racialized view of the world that put whiteness at the center and denied the class movement. But this nationalist class, critiqued by Frantz Fanon in terms of pitfalls of national consciousness in his book *The Wretched of the Earth*, did not come into leadership of the new states as an independent bourgeoisie: It was soon ensnared in neocolonialism, cold-war politics, and globalization. It was a class with no capital, no inventors among its members, no new worlds to conquer and rob—only a world in which to beg and a nation to rob. During the anticolonial struggle this class saw its power as derived from the people; and after independence, as derived from a cozy relationship with the Western bourgeoisie.

The Pan-Africanism that envisaged the ideal of wholeness was gradually cut down to the size of a continent, then a nation, a region, an ethnos, a clan, and even a village in some instances. Lacking a fundamental reorganization of production and a change in view of the sources of its power, the African middle class became merely an enabler of the easy flow of national resources from Africa to the West, with a lucrative commission fee for its role as a middleman. The European bourgeoisie stole from the colonies and from each other, raiding each other's ships in the high seas: The African middle class uses the ship of state to loot the nation. Fragmented economically, its leaders pawning her resources, Africa remains the younger, poorer relation of global capitalism.

The European middle class had the vigor and energy of youth; the African middle class became as senile as Afriga the frog in Kwei Armah's novel, *The Beautyful Ones Are Not Yet Born*. Indeed, senility set in before it ever experienced the vigor and daring of youth: In "its beginnings, the national bourgeoisie of the colonial countries identifies itself with the decadence of the bourgeoisie of the West."[14] The European bourgeoisie in its youth took charge of its own and raided others to augment its national coffers; the African bourgeoisie raids its own treasures to augment Western treasuries. This contrast is clearest when we consider the two groups' different attitudes toward their most important heritage: languages.

The two salient features of the European Renaissance are discovery and recovery. By *discovery* I don't mean the voyages of exploration and conquests or the creation of colonial otherness but, rather, Europe's encounter with its own languages. Erich Auerbach describes the European Renaissance as "the movement through which the literary languages of the various European peoples finally shook off Latin."[15] Before this, Latin had occupied a position not too dissimilar from that occupied by European languages in Africa today: "[I]t was virtually the sole vehicle of intellectual life and written communication . . . a foreign language that had to be learned . . . cut off from the spoken language."[16] Overwhelmed by the pervasive presence of Latin, the pioneers of this shift were at first apologetic, time and again finding it necessary (much like Nuala Ni Dhomhnaill in the case of her choice of Irish) to answer the question as to why they wrote in the vernacular. For Dante, writing in *Del Vulgari Eloquentia* about two kinds of speech, the foreign and the vernacular, "the vernacular is the nobler, both because it is enjoyed by the whole world (though it has been divided into [languages with] differing words and paradigms), and because it is natural to us, while the other is more an artificial product."[17] He defends his choice of the Italian of Tuscany as the language of critical commentary, on the basis of its being the language of his primary experience. "And since the better known a route is, the more safely and more quickly it may be traveled, I shall proceed only along that language which is my own, leaving aside the others."[18] Regarding Italian as compared to other languages he finds that "each thing naturally desires its own self-preservation; so if the vernacular could have any desires of its own, it would desire to be preserved."[19] He rejected calls by one of his humanistic friends, Giovanni del Virgilio, to abandon the limited audience of a writer in vernacular and seek learned fame and immortality as a Latin poet. In response, Dante explained why he did not write in Latin, likening his vernacular to a "ewe who can hardly carry her udders, so filled they are with milk . . . I am getting ready to milk her with skilled hands."[20] He wrote this response in perfect Latin, as if to show that he could compose in it, if he so chose, but he had consciously opted for his Italian.

In time, European intellectuals of every nation embraced their own languages with pride. By 1518, Martin Luther could look to his fellow native Germans and thank God "that I hear and find my God in the German language in a way which I have not found Him up to now in the Latin, Greek, or Hebrew tongues."[21] And speakers of English went from seeing the language as ineloquent, raw, crude, barbarous,[22] and incapable of expressing scientific and literary thought with the precision and elegance of Latin to embracing it as elegant, eloquent, and capable of handling all thought. Some, like Samuel Daniel, even started describing it as the nation's best glory, a future export to the world.

> *And who, in time, knows whether we may vent [export]*
> *The treasure of our tongue, to what strange shores*
> *This gaine of our best glory shall be sent*
> *T'inrich unknowing Nations with our stores?*
> *What worlds in th'yet unformed Occident*
> *May come refin'd with th' accents that are ours?*[23]

Allied to this discovery was the Europeans' recovery of classical knowledge, thereby resurrecting the ancients as com-
panions to the present—as illustrated in Dante's choice of
Virgil as his guide through the Inferno. Or in Machiavelli's
letter in 1513 explaining how the ancients were his daily com-
panions during the writing of *The Prince:* Upon coming
home in the evening, he would take off his everyday clothes,
put on "the robes of court and palace, and in this graver dress
I enter the courts of the ancients and am welcomed by them,
and there I taste the food that alone is mine and for which I
was born. And there I make bold to speak to them and ask
the motives of their actions, and they, in their humanity, reply to me."[24]

An almost identical evocation of the ancients can be found
in a passage by Montaigne, who writes how Plutarch "in-
trudeth himselfe into your work, and gently reacheth you a
helpe-affording hand, fraught with rare embellishments, and
inexhaustible of precious riches."[25] And Philemon Holland
talks of Livius as a living person with "something to say that
might be vital to England's destiny"; he asks Queen Elizabeth
to "reach forth your gracious hand to T. Livius" and allow him
"to live under your princely protection."[26] In England, says
Matthiessen, "the classical past became so vivid that it seemed
to some minds almost more real than the present."[27] Recov-
ering from the past and recouping knowledge from contemporaries become a passion, a duty to one's own language.

It is the art of translation that largely makes such recovery possible. This is how the world of the ancients became part of the European Renaissance's present. Indeed, the impact of translations on the development of European languages and cultures is enormous, both in the broad cultural sense as a function of imitation and emulation and in the narrow linguistic sense whereby translation becomes an art of naturalizing the ancients such that they become speakers of modern European languages—as if the ancient texts were written in the modern. For instance, Martin Luther's translation of the bible was seen as having brought about modern German. Jane Newman writes of German language societies that sprung up after Luther; they looked back to him, a century later, as the one who had "planted sweetness, dignity, and suppleness to our language."[28] William Tyndale, in talking about his incentive for translating the bible into English, expressed sentiments similar to Luther's in relation to English: "I had perceived by experience, how that it was impossible to establish the lay people in any truth, except the scripture were plainly laid before their eyes in their mother tongue, that they might see the process, order and meaning of the text."[29] Through translations both men introduced their mother tongues into the community of holy languages.[30] Reformation as a whole could be seen as that which brought the various European languages into the family of holy languages of

Hebrew, Latin, and Greek, for each of these languages could now lead the nationals directly to God. God understood vernacular.

Translations were not only from Latin and Greek but also from other European languages. In England, a nation that, according to Matthiessen, had grown conscious of its cultural inferiority to the continent, "suddenly burned with the desire to excel its rivals in letters, as well as in ships and gold."[31] Translations were the means of effecting the desired excellence. "The translator's work was an act of patriotism. He, too, as well as the voyager and merchant, could do some good for his country: he believed that foreign books were just as important for England's destiny as the discoveries of her seamen, and he brought them into his native speech with all the enthusiasm of a conquest."[32]

Through original productions and translations the vernaculars grew, and though they had met with resistance, the kind we see in Africa today, by the end of the sixteenth century their victorious emergence from the shadow of Latin was complete. Consider the exuberance of language that we find in Rabelais, Shakespeare, and Cervantes: These are writers who discovered the limitless expressive power of their languages, writers who reveled in the possibilities they saw in their rediscovered tongues. In their journey of emancipation, the languages had moved from diffidence, imitation, and emulation to self-confident readiness, thus surpassing and subjugating other tongues and cultures. The "I gave you language" line in Prospero's admonition to Caliban in Shakespeare's *The Tempest* proceeded from the confident climax of the European Renaissance, a climax that unfortunately was also the beginning of Africa's dismemberment.

No renaissance, however, can replicate all aspects of another; but all contain the central idea of rebirth and the spring of a new vision of being. Re-membering Africa is the only way of ensuring Africa's own full rebirth from the dark ages into which it was plunged by the European Renaissance, Enlightenment, and modernity. The success of Africa's renaissance depends on its commitment and ability to remember itself, guided by the great re-membering vision of Pan-Africanism. This idea has already served Africa well—inspiring, as it has done, Afro-modernity. But it is a flawed modernity for, among other things, it has yielded several nation-states founded on colonial boundaries that perpetuate the Berlin-based divisions, with the result that even people of the same language, culture, and history remain citizens of different states. These states, in turn, often erect insurmountable barriers in the movement of peoples, goods, businesses, and services.

But Pan-Africanism has not outlived its mission. Seen as an economic, political, cultural, and psychological re-membering vision, it should continue to guide remembering practices. Economic Pan-Africanism will translate into a network of communications—air, sea, land, telephone, Internet—that ease intracontinental movements of peoples, goods, businesses, and services. Africa becomes a power bloc able to negotiate on an equal basis with all other global economies. But this is impossible without a powerful political union, as championed by Kwame Nkrumah. Pan-Africanism has to translate into a United States of Africa with the African union transformed from a union of African heads of state into a genuine union of African peoples. Political Pan-Africanism should make the continent a base where African peoples, meaning continentals and people of African descent, can feel truly at home—a realization of the Garveysian vision of Africa for Africans, both at home and abroad. Such an Africa would be a secure base where all peoples of African descent can feel inspired to visit, invest, and even live if they so choose. But we are still far away from this. Instead, as a result of famines, massacres, denials of rights, insecurity, and intolerance— replicas of colonial times—virtually every African state is hosting refugees from its neighbors and citizens continue to flee from the continent altogether—a "brain drain" that is much talked about. In this sense *African renaissance* means, first and foremost, the economic and political recovery of the continent's power, as enshrined in the vision of Pan-Africanism.

But this can be brought about effectively only through a collective self-confidence enabled by the resurrection of African memory, which in turn calls for a fundamental change in attitude towards African languages on the part of the African bourgeoisie, the African governments, and the African intellectual community.

Diasporic African communities must try to add an African language to their cultural arsenal. For though the diasporic African has a new mother tongue, he can reach out to his African memory only by making efforts to learn an African language to add to, not replace, what he already speaks. In so doing he would be connecting himself to the means of the memory that has sustained him for so long in his struggles to find himself in a world that constantly puts barriers in his way. But the challenge is primarily one for those on the continent: to produce for Africa in African languages, because language is the basic re-membering practice—though it is often missing in discussions about intellectual and literary movements from negritude to Afro-centrism.

In fact, there has been an unbroken tradition of writing in African languages that goes all the way back to Timbuctoo in the twelfth century (even earlier in Egypt and Ethiopia) and continues to the present day. Mazisi Kunene, who even in exile continued to write in Zulu, can trace his literary ancestry in an unbroken line back to the *imbongi* (oral poets) of the

Shaka court in the nineteenth century. Even when European languages had begun to seduce the minds of African graduates of colonial and missionary schools, there were some among them who argued against complete surrender to the seduction. Such was the case of S.E.K. Mqhayi, who at the dawn of the twentieth century argued for African languages against those South African intellectuals who thought that English was the best means of experiencing the modern. Ntongela Masilela's work on the intellectual history of South Africa places Mqhayi's work at the center of the early phases of the genesis of Afro-modernity. "His unyielding stand on the historic question of whether the English language or the African languages should be the instrument of representation in modernity defined in many ways the literary issue of South African modernity in the twentieth century,"[33] writes Masilela. Practicing what he argued out in theory, Mqhayi wrote in IsiXhosa, generating what some intellectuals even then gave the name of *renaissance*. Indeed, they praised him for standing up "for our language and by pen and word of mouth created a Renaissance in our literature."[34] In the continent as a whole, the anticolonial resistance that climaxed in the emergence of several independent states also generated and, in turn, was reflected in a plethora of poems, songs, and newspapers in African languages. In Kenya all of these were banned by the colonial state, followed by casualties among

the writers themselves: A partial list includes Gakaara Wan-
jau, who was imprisoned; Henry Muoria, who was exiled; and
Stanley Kagĩka, who was killed. Other examples of continuity of writing in African languages include Amharic in
Ethiopia and Kiswahili in Kenya, Uganda, and Tanzania.
Swahili literature in East Africa follows an unbroken line
from Muyaka to Abdilatif Abdalla.

What happened in the 1950s, with the dawn of independence—when, under the neocolonial context of that independence, Europhone writing came to be considered the
norm—was therefore a deviation from this veritable tradition. African languages and literature are not dead, have
never died; it's just that the house they built was taken over
by European languages, which act as though the African languages are corpses that will not rise from the dead to claim
their house. The deviation, like the Anglophonic takeover of
the identity of Irish literature, has taken on the mantle and
identity of African literature. But this claim has not been
without a challenge, the most celebrated being that of Obi
Wali in the 1960s, when he wrote in Volume 10 of the journal
Transition that Europhone-African literature was coming to
a dead end, and that it would be just as ridiculous to describe as "African literature" works written by Africans in
non-African languages as to describe as "French literature"
works written in Yoruba by Frenchmen. (The most popular

of my own works of nonfiction is *Decolonising the Mind*,
which continues the same theme.) As a result of those chal-
lenges and the ensuing debates about the nature of the deviation and memory burial, there are indications of a return to
the venerable tradition of Mqhayi, Fagunwa, Gakaara, Mazisi
Kunene, and Abdilatif Abdalla—a visible but agonizingly
slow movement whereby African languages are claiming back
the title and ownership of the house they built. Some intellectuals and governments alike are beginning to pay attention.

In the year 2000, a number of African scholars and writers
met in Eritrea and came up with the *Asmara Declaration on
African Languages and Literatures,* a ten-point document that
begins by calling on African languages to take on the duty,
challenge, and responsibility of speaking for the continent. It
then lists nine other conditions—including recognition of
the vitality, equality, and diversity of African languages as a basis for the future empowerment of African peoples; the necessity of communication among African languages and their
development at all levels of the schooling system; promotion
of research, science, and technology in African languages;
and the necessity of democracy and gender equality in the development of African languages—and it concludes by em-
phasizing that African languages are essential for the
decolonization of African minds as well as for the African
renaissance.

The declaration called upon all African states, the OAU, the United Nations, and all international organizations that serve Africa to join the effort to recognize and support African languages, hopefully making the declaration itself the basis of new policies. It has since been translated into several African languages.

Some African governments are grappling with the reality of multiple languages and have taken specific stances on this matter. Most are still vague about it. But recently, during its sixth ordinary session in Khartoum, the African Union (AU), successor to the OAU, underlined the importance of African languages as instrumental tools for education and culture, development and progress, by establishing an African Academy for Languages as a specialized office of the AU seated in Bamako, the capital of Mali. In the same sixth ordinary session, the AU decided to declare 2006 the Year of African Languages. These are important symbolic steps in the right direction, but it is worth noting that in its previous life as the OAU, the organization had a cultural charter that lauded the centrality of African languages in modernization. Unfortunately the charter remained on paper. The hope is that the current AU position will move from paper to the ground and that all years—not just 2006—will be declared years of African languages.

But how do a thousand tongues, barely mutually comprehensible among themselves nationally, speak for a continent? Would Africa become a house of Babel? Would the multiplicity of African languages within and between states merely exacerbate the fragmentation of the continent? In a continent where postindependence has seen wars of secession in Nigeria, Somalia, Congo, and Ethiopia, such prospects are nightmarish. But it is also important to remember that those civil wars were not fought on language lines. In the case of Somalia, with its single-language history, the many-languages argument is an absurdity. But even if it were a factor in the conflicts, a multiplicity of languages in Africa would not be any worse or better than the multiplicity of languages in Asia and Europe.

The fear of exacerbating divisions along language lines is obviously genuine—but the solution is not to continue burying the languages and the means of African memory under a Europhonic paradise. On the contrary, as noted in point nine of the Asmara Declaration, the solution lies in translation.

Though translation has long had a bad name, dating back to the Platonic dialogues where the name of Hermes, the god who invented language and speech, is said to signify his being "an interpreter or a messenger or thief or liar, or bargainer,"[35] it has nonetheless played a crucial role in the development of many societies. Marxian texts that have inspired many social revolutions were read by their adherents in translation. Many words and phrases in the works of Lenin and Mao, passionately debated in classrooms and political platforms all over the world, are known only in translation. And we have already seen the role of translation in the European Renaissance and the emergence of capitalist modernity. It was the translation of the ninety-five Lutheran theses that launched reformation, with the bible itself coming to play a significant role in the development of European languages.

Indeed, the bible has played almost the same role in African culture as in European culture—an observation that brings us to an ironic dichotomy: On the one hand Europe suffocated and helped starve African languages, while on the other hand the necessity for religious conversion compelled Europe to maintain the written tradition of African languages. Missionary presses enabled some of the writings in African languages. But given the editorial censorship that did not want these writings to carry instances of anticolonial resistance, what the presses produced were often starved of content, leaving only that which served the needs of anthropology with its interest, at the time, in static pasts or that which pointed to the means of Africans' conversion from themselves. Still, their translations of the bible and other tracts into African languages played a role that cannot be ignored, and they share credit in keeping alive the literary retention of African languages.

Translation is the language of languages, a language through which all languages can talk to one another. Thus, for a writer, given that translation between African languages can cement the heritages that are shared by the languages, the entire continent, with its vast African language audiences, becomes a potential market. Through translations of works written directly in African languages, a shared modern heritage will emerge. But apart from aiding conversation among contemporary African languages, translation will benefit the African renaissance. This is the theme of the next chapter, in which I describe South Africa as a microcosm of the black and African experience.

One of the greatest sons of Africa, Kweggyr Aggrey, used to tell the story of a farmer who brought up an eagle among the chickens. The eagle grew up behaving like a chicken and believing he was a chicken. One day a hunter visited the farmer and an argument ensued as to whether the eagle could remember who he was. The farmer was absolutely sure that he had turned the eagle into a chicken. The hunter asked whether he could try to revive the eagle's memory. On the first day, he was unable to make him fly beyond the distance that chickens can manage. I told you, says the farmer: I have turned him into a chicken. On the second day, the same disappointment occurred, with the eagle flying a few yards and then diving downward, earthbound. I told you he cannot remember, says the farmer in triumph: He walks like a chicken and thinks like a chicken; he will never fly. The hunter does not give up. On the third day, he takes the eagle atop a hill and talks to him, pointing his eyes to the sky and reminding him that he is an eagle. And then it happened. Looking at the limitless immensity of the blue skies above, the eagle flapped his wings, raised himself, and then up he soared, flying toward the azure.

The African eagle can fly only with his re-membered wings. Re-membering Africa will bring about the flowering of the African renaissance; and Afro-modernity will play its role in the globe on the reciprocal egalitarian basis of give and take, ultimately realizing the Garveysian vision of a common humanity of progress and achievement "that will wipe away the odor of prejudice, and elevate the human race to the height of real godly love and satisfaction."[36]

CHAPTER FOUR

FROM COLOR TO SOCIAL CONSCIOUSNESS

South Africa in the Black Imagination[1]

When Vasco da Gama set foot on the Cape in 1498, he did so during the period that came to be known as the European Renaissance, the founding moment of capitalist modernity and Western bourgeois ascendancy in the world. It was also the beginning of the wanton destruction of many city civilizations along the coasts of Africa, East Africa in particular. In 1994 Nelson Mandela, as the first black president of the Republic of South Africa, recalled the destruction of Carthage by the generals of an earlier empire when he said: "[W]here South Africa appears on the agenda again, let it be because we want to discuss what its contribution shall be to the making of the new African Renaissance. Let it be because we want to discuss what materials it will supply for the rebuilding of the African city of Carthage."[2] In a sense, South

Africa has already supplied such material by way of the men and women whose lives and actions and thoughts have made South Africa an integral part of the black self-imagination. Steve Biko, the inspiration of the lecture on which this chapter is based, is one among several in this great gallery whose work and devotion have impacted people beyond the native shores and made it possible for us to even talk about the emergence of a new Africa out of the colonial ashes of the latter-day empires.

Steve Biko combines the cultural, the intellectual, and the political in the same person. And he exemplifies the public intellectual in its finest tradition. In one of his interviews reproduced in *I Write What I Like,* Biko describes a confrontation with his jailors in which he asserts his right to resistance for as long as he is able: *"If you guys want to do this your way,"* he tells his jailors, *"you have got to handcuff me and bind my feet together, so that I can't respond. If you allow me to respond, I'm certainly going to respond. And I'm afraid you may have to kill me in the process even if it's not your intention."*[3] These words, spoken in 1976 a few months before Biko's brutal murder, are evocative of others spoken earlier in 1964 by Mandela from the dock at the Rivonia Trial where, in expressing his ideal of a democratic and free society, he reaffirmed his commitment to live for and achieve that ideal: "But if it needs be it is an ideal for which I am prepared to die."[4] Mandela eventually went to prison for twenty-seven years; Biko died in prison, having written his own epitaph: *"It is better to die for an idea that lives than to live for an idea that dies."*[5] In both cases, the words and the lives that were lived added up to a rich intellectual legacy of African heroes and heroines of Pan-African struggles, a legacy summed up in Robert Sobukwe's words: *"It is meet that we tell the truth before we die."*[6] One associates Sobukwe and Biko with consciousness, Mandela with renaissance. But it is significant for me that all three men—while inextricably linked to black and social imagination everywhere—came from South Africa, where their concepts of consciousness and renaissance have now found new life.

As a Kenyan, an African, and a writer, I attribute a good part of my social experience and intellectual formation to South Africa. I had just started primary school when it was announced that one of our teachers—from my village, moreover—was leaving us. He was going to Fort Hare for more learning. The image of Fort Hare as a mecca of learning was reinforced when later yet another from the same region, this time a minister of religion, followed suit. However, it was while I was a student in an Independent African School that I first became aware that the South African story was my story also. The independent African-run schools in Kenya were started in the 1930s, their coming into being inspired by the Ethiopian Movement in South, Central, and East Africa.[7] But it was the way our teacher taught the South African story, from the perspective of the black experience, that brought it home to us, and the names of Shaka, Moshoeshoe, and Cetewayo became part of our collective memory. When the Mau Mau war for Kenya's independence started in 1952, the colonial administration reacted by closing down these schools or taking them over, so as to turn the story of South Africa into that of Vasco da Gama, Kruger and the Great Trek, and of course General Smuts.

Fortunately, the other image—of the South African story as my story—never disappeared. It was rekindled, in fact, with an even greater intensity when later in high school, a missionary-run school, I happened to see one of the only two African teachers there holding a copy of Peter Abrahams's *Tell Freedom*. It is difficult to fully describe the impact of that title on my imagination, encountering it, as I did, when Kenya was in the midst of the War for Independence. The title led me to the works of Abrahams and to the great gallery of South African writers, some of whom I would later interact with as fellow writers and friends. I cannot forget the influence of Es'kia Mphahlele on African writing in general and on Kenyan writing in particular. His Chemchemi Cultural Center in Nairobi in the early years of our independence truly became a fountain of inspiration for young Kenyan talent. His struggles for the African image as that of an assertive sovereign subject, acting on his environment, resonated within me—growing up, as I did, in the shadow of the colonial white image of the African as an object without agency, always acted upon. By exploring human interiority, South African writers (as well as artists and musicians) told the human dimension about what was being enacted in the open theater of organized politics, which had also produced the heroes and heroines who became expressions of our own struggles. I cannot think of another country that has produced so many writers who have become part of the African experience by using the term *African* to the same degree of pregnant inclusiveness as Thabo Mbeki did in his 1996 address to the constitutional assembly: "I am an African."[8]

Not surprisingly, South Africa is always on my mind. At the UNICEF conference on the situation of children in Southern Africa held in Harare in March 1988, I began my lecture on the role of intellectual workers[9] with the assertion that the liberation of South Africa was the key to the social liberation of the continent. Later, in April 1990, in an article celebrating the release of Nelson Mandela,[10] I came back to the same theme—the place of South Africa in the black self-imagination—and argued that South Africa was a mirror of the emergence of the

modern world. I was not saying anything new. No less a figure than Adam Smith of *The Wealth of Nations*[11] fame cited
the discovery of America and that of a passage to the East Indies by way of the Cape of Good Hope as the two greatest
and most important events recorded in human history—a
claim repeated in the nineteenth century by Marx and Engels
in *The Communist Manifesto,* where they argue that these
twin events gave to commerce, navigation, and industry an
impulse never before known, leading rapidly to a revolutionary element in the tottering feudal society.[12]

Smith wondered about the benefits or misfortunes that
could follow these events. Having lived through the consequences, we now know that the benefits went largely to Europe and America, the colonizing nations. The misfortunes
devolved on Africa, and on the colonized peoples.

Whereas Smith wondered about possible benefits and
misfortunes, Marx and Engels were certain that the dialecti-
cally linked benefits and misfortunes of capitalist modernity
would create a world that reflected the West. In forcing all nations, on pain of extinction, to partake of that modernity, the
European bourgeoisie "compels them to introduce what it
calls civilization into their midst. . . . In one word, it creates
a world after its own image."[13] The creation of a world after
the image of the Western bourgeoisie was not without resistance, as seen in class and national struggles everywhere.

Because of its historical constitution, South Africa—more intensely than most nations—embodied the consequences of the benefits to a white minority linked to Europe and the misfortunes to the majority linked to the rest of Africa and Asia. The minority Europeans tried to create a South Africa after their own image, which they, too, saw as representative of Western civilization. But South Africa would also embody the resistance against the negative consequences of that modernity; indeed, in its history we see clashes and interactions of race, class, gender, ethnicity, and religion—social forces that bedevil the world today.

As a site of concentration of both domination and resistance, South Africa mirrored the worldwide struggles between capital and labor and between the colonizer and the colonized. For Africa, let's face it, South African history—from Vasco da Gama's landing at the Cape in 1498 to its liberation in 1994—frames all modern social struggles, and certainly black struggles. If the struggle, often fought with swords, between racialized capital and racialized labor was about wealth and power, it was also a battle over images often fought with words. When Biko asserted the right to "write what I like," he was asserting the right to draw the image of himself, unfettered—a position reflecting Robert Sobukwe's description of the African struggle as that for the right to call our souls our own.

Images are very important. Most people like looking at themselves in the mirror. Most like to have their photos taken. In many African societies the shadow was thought to carry the soul of a person. But here we are talking about the image of the world as a physical, economic, political, moral, and intellectual universe of our being. This image resides in memory where also dwell dreams and our conception of life.

Colonialism tried to control the memory of the colonized; or, rather, in the words of Caribbean thinker Sylvia Wynter, it tried to subject the colonized to its memory, to make the colonized see themselves through the hegemonic memory of the colonizing center. Put another way, the colonizing presence sought to induce a historical amnesia on the colonized by mutilating the memory of the colonized; and where that failed, it dismembered it, and then tried to re-member it to the colonizer's memory—to his way of defining the world, including his take on the nature of the relations between colonizer and colonized.

This relation was primarily economic. The colonized as worker, as peasant, produces for another. His land and his labor benefit another. This arrangement was, of course, effected through power, political power, but it was also accomplished through cultural subjugation—for instance, through control of the education system. The ultimate goal was to establish psychic dominance on the part of the colonizer and psychic subservience on the part of the colonized.

The acts and consequences of economic and political subjugation are obvious, for you cannot persuade a person who has lost her land to forget the loss, the person who goes hungry to forget the hunger, and the person who bears the whiplashes of an unjust system to forget the pain. But cultural subjugation is more dangerous, because it is more subtle and its effects longer lasting. Moreover, it can cause a person who has lost her land, who feels the pangs of hunger, who carries flagellated flesh, to look at those experiences differently. It can lead to a pessimism that fails to see in her history any positive lessons in dealings with the present. Such a person has been drained of the historical memory of a different world. The prophet who once warned "Fear not those who kill the body but those who kill the spirit" was right on the mark; certainly Steve Biko, with his black consciousness, was working within that prophetic warning.

Consciousness distinguishes humans from the rest of nature. In humans, death is marked by the end of consciousness. In that sense all humans, to the extent that they are human, have a consciousness. But in a situation of the colonizer and the colonized, the question of consciousness is vital; in fact, it becomes a site of intense struggle. Let me fall back on Hegel. In his books, particularly *The Phenomenology of Spirit* and *The Science of Logic*, Hegel distinguishes between Being-in-itself, not the Kantian unknowable thing-in-itself, and Being-for-itself. Being-in-itself is mere existence. Being-for-itself is

Being aware not only of its existence but of existence for a purpose, an ethical purpose—the distinction between saying "I live to eat" and "I eat to live." But in a situation of master and slave, the *for-itself* can be appropriated by another, to become the *for-another*.

Marx applied the same notion to classes and class struggle, distinguishing between a class-in-itself and a class-for-itself, whereby the latter becomes aware of itself as a class with its own class interests and identity. The struggle of classes takes the form of the dominant trying to turn the dominated not into a class for itself but, rather, into a class for the interests of another, the dominating. In race politics, the same can apply when the self-consciousness of a race is appropriated by another to serve the interests of a dominant race. Racism was a conscious class ideology of imperialism, and of colonialism and colonial relations; even clearly economic and political matters often came wrapped in race. The problem of the twentieth century, said W.E.B. Dubois, was the color line: "the relation of the darker to the lighter races of men in Asia and Africa, in America and the islands of the sea." The more class-conscious C.L.R. James would add that the race question was subsidiary to the class question in politics and that thinking of imperialism in terms of race was disastrous. "But to neglect the racial factor as merely incidental is an error only less grave than to make it fundamental."[14] Within the overall context of economic and political domination, race *could, was,* and *is* often used as a means of diminishing the self-evaluation of the dominated. In that context, racial self-assertion was a necessary first step in the reclamation of a positive self-awareness. A people without a consciousness of their Being in the World, to use the Heideggerian phrase, can easily be guided by another to wherever the guide wants to take him, even to his own extinction.

Black consciousness then becomes the right of black peoples to draw an image of themselves that negates and transcends the image of themselves that was drawn by those who would weaken them in their fight for, and assertion of, their humanity—or, in the Sobukwean formulation, to fight for the right to call our souls our own. It seeks to draw the image of a possible world, different from and transcending the one drawn by the West, by reconnecting itself to different historical memories and dreams; and that is why, in the Preface to the 1996 edition of Biko's book *I Write What I Like,* Bishop Tutu makes a tantalizing connection between consciousness and renaissance. "It is good that there is this new edition to enable us to savor the inspired words of Steve Biko—perhaps it could just spark a black renaissance."[15] Here Tutu intimates that positive self-consciousness can open new vistas and extensions of our being. But consciousness resides in memory. Even at the very simple level of our daily experience we get excited when we visit, say, the place where we were born, and recall the various landmarks of our childhood. The first thing Mandela did after leaving Robben Island was to go straight back to the house in Soweto where he used to live before his incarceration twenty-seven years before. Sometimes we feel a sense of loss when we find that the place no longer holds any traces of what it once meant to us. A loss of memory is a real loss of those traces that enable individuals to make sense of what is happening to them.

Torture, imprisonment, and isolation are all attempts at breaking the connection with memory. This fact was vividly brought home to us when at the Cape waterfront, Tokyo Segxale pointed to Robben Island, where he had been imprisoned for eighteen years. Robben Island brings to mind another island, St. Helena, where Dinizulu, Cetewayo's son,[16] and his lieutenants were imprisoned for their role in the Zulu anticolonial resistance of 1887–1888. What saved the Robben Island prisoners from the fate of Dinizulu—and, earlier, of Napoleon—Tokyo said reflectively, was the fact that they could see the land in the distance. It was not of course just the land. It was also the memory the land held—the memory, in their case, of a continuously struggling people, all the way back to the Khoi and San nations and their defeat of the Portuguese army under Admiral Almeida. In short, the land they could see and the memory it carried compelled them to resist Robben Island's attempt to rob them of their spirit. Memory as the site of dreams, and of desire, is thus crucial to the construction of our being. But if memory is the site of dreams, desire, image, consciousness, where is memory's location? Memory resides in language and is clarified by language. By incorporating the colonial world into the international capitalist order and relations, with itself as the center of such order and relations, the imperialist West also subjected the rest of the world to its memory through a vast naming system. It planted its memory on our landscape. Egoli became Johannesburg. The great East African Lake, known by the Luo people as Namlolwe, became Lake Victoria. The plantation of their memory on our landscape was brought home to me when yesterday our hosts took us to Eastern Cape. I was very excited about the visit, for the region has produced some of the greatest names in Africa's intellectual and political history. It was the region from which came Tiyo Soga, William Gqoba, Pambani Jeremiah Mzimba, Charlotte Manye Maxeke, Elijah Makiwane, W. B. Rubusana, John Knox Bokwe, Mqhayi, Sobukwe, Biko, Mbeki, and Mandela—to mention only a few. But these were not the names that we found pointing to the identity of the landscape. Instead we encountered King Williams Town, Queens Town, Port Elizabeth, East London, Berlin, Hamburg, Frankfurt, Stutterheim, and Ginsberg—a clear case of conquerors writing their own memory on the landscape of our resistance memory. They also planted their memory on our bodies. Ngũgĩ became James. Noliwe became Margaret. Our names got stuck with their names. Thus our bodies, in terms of their self-definition, became forever branded by their memory. The name-mark pointing to my body defines my identity. James? And I answer: Yes, I am. And, most important, they planted their memory on our intellect through language. Language and the culture it carries are the most crucial parts of that naming system by which Europe subjected the colonized to its memory. The more educated the colonial subjects are in the culture of the colonizer, the more severe the subjection, with devastating results for the community of subjects as a whole.

Writers, artists, musicians, intellectuals, and workers in ideas are the keepers of memory of a community. What fate awaits a community when its keepers of memory have been subjected to the West's linguistic means of production and storage of memory—English, French, and Portuguese—such that those who should have been keepers of the sacred word now see themselves, and the different possibilities for the community, only within the linguistic boundaries of memory incorporated? We have languages, but our keepers of memory feel that they cannot store knowledge, emotions, and intellect in African languages. It is like possessing a granary but, at harvest, storing your produce in somebody else's granary.

The result is that 90 percent of intellectual production in Africa is stored in European languages, a continuation of the colonial project in which not even a single treaty between Europe and Africa exists in any African language. So, look for Africa in African languages and you will not find her.

The relationship between African and European languages as producers and stores of memory have been at the heart of the struggle for a sovereign consciousness. It has certainly been part of the South African intellectual tradition since the rise of what scholar Ntongela Masilela calls the "New African Movement."[17]

In *The South African Outlook* dated July 1, 1939, there is a Letter to the Editor written by B. W. Vilakazi.[18] It is a reply to his friend and fellow writer H.I.E. Dhlomo, the younger of the two Dhlomos and the author of *The Valley of a Thousand Hills*. H.I.E. Dhlomo wrote largely in English, in contrast to his elder brother R.R.R. Dhlomo, who wrote in Zulu. H.I.E. Dhlomo had published an article on African drama and poetry in which he disagreed with Vilakazi's theory of the rhyme system in Zulu poetry developed from Vilakazi's master's thesis, "The Conception and Development of Poetry in Zulu." Whereas Dhlomo draws from Hebrew writings and Shakespeare and quotes liberally from Western sources including Sir Arthur Quiller-Couch to buttress his argument, Vilakazi turns tables to remind Dhlomo that he does not write in Zulu, thus aligning himself subtly with the elder Dhlomo. Vilakazi is clearly unapologetic in his building on the literary heritage of Zulu language in form and content:

> My course primarily lies in Zulu poetry. And there I am definite. Zulu poetry is a contribution to Zulu Literature. Secondly, I am convinced it is a mission, a self-imposed mission, to help build a vista of Bantu poetry. And Zulu poetry will therefore stand parallel to English, German or Italian poetry, all of which form the realm of what is called European poetry.[19]

In saying that Zulu is part of Bantu literature and that *Bantu poetry stands parallel to European poetry,* Vilakazi is arguing that Zulu or any African language is to African literature what any particular European language is to European literature. He recognizes that there is no abstract African literature that is not rooted in specific African languages any more than there is an abstract European literature that is not rooted in specific European languages. And he is very clear about what he means by Bantu literature:

> By Bantu drama, I mean a drama written by a Bantu, for the Bantu, in a Bantu language. I do not class English or Afrikaans dramas on Bantu themes, whether

or not these are written by Black people. I do not call
them contributions to Bantu Literature. It is the same
with poetry.[20]

And then follows a statement that is a celebration of Vilakazi's refusal to be subjected to the linguistic perimeters of
European memory.

> I have an unshaken belief in the possibilities of Bantu
> Languages and their Dramas, provided the Bantu
> writers *themselves* [original emphasis] can learn to
> love their languages, and use them as vehicles for
> thought, feeling and will. After all, the belief, resulting
> in literature, is a demonstration of people's "self"
> where they cry: "Ego quad sum." That is our pride in
> being black and we cannot change creation.[21]

Is this not a literary expression of black consciousness
long before Biko gave it a name and currency?

Vilakazi's conscious commitment to African languages
takes us back to Krune Mqhayi. In his book *Long Walk to
Freedom*, Mandela describes an event at his school, Healdtown, that for him was "'like a comet streaking across the
night sky.' It was a visit by Mqhayi. Performing on the stage
in his native Xhosa dress and holding an assegai, he tells his

mesmerized audience: 'The assegai stands for what is glorious and true in African history; it is a symbol of the African as a warrior and the African as an artist,' and contrasts this to skillful but soulless Europe.... What I am talking to you about is not the overlapping of one culture over another; what I am talking about is the brutal clash between what is indigenous and good and what is foreign and bad.... We cannot allow these foreigners who do not care for our culture to take over our nation. I predict that one day, the forces of African society will achieve a momentous victory over the interloper."[22] The performance profoundly impacted the young Mandela's previous assumptions about white and black power: "I could hardly believe my ears. His boldness in speaking of such delicate matters in the presence of Dr. Wellington and other whites seemed utterly astonishing to us. Yet at the same time, it aroused and motivated us, and began to alter my perception of men like Dr. Wellington whom I had considered as my benefactor."[23] But Mqhayi's performance with its unapologetic celebration of being both Xhosa and African did something more as well: It showed that there is no such a thing as an abstract African, and it led the young Mandela to accept his own Xhosa-Being as the real condition of his African-Being and not the other way around.

Mqhayi wrote in Xhosa, and in the *Bantu World* dated July 20, 1935 (the same year in which the event narrated by Mandela took place), another South African intellectual, Guybon

B. Sinxo, wrote a commissioned piece on Mqhayi in which among other tributes he described Mqhayi's book, *Ityala Lama Wele,* as being second only to the bible in greatness. And of Mqhayi who learnt under the feet of Xhosa elders, he wrote:

> To-day . . . that same boy who at a time when most of the educated Africans in the Cape as well as Europeans controlling Native Education looked down upon Xhosa stood up for our language and by pen and word of mouth created a Renaissance in our literature.

Indeed, it was in banner headlines devised by the sub-editor R. V. Selope Thema that the July 20, 1935, issue of *Bantu World* carried this tribute to Mqhayi as a creator of Xhosa renaissance.

On reflection, what stand out are not only this whole-hearted tribute by two fellow intellectuals, Sinxo, a Xhosa; and Thema, a Pedi; but also the fact that the term *renaissance* is used in 1935 in reference to the work of an African intellectual who wrote in an African language and whose performance in that language had a profound impact on the Healdtown students. From their tributes Mqhayi emerges as a renaissance figure combining many talents and interests: a performer, writer, poet, dramatist, essayist, translator, humorist, critic, cultural advocate, and political analyst; a public intellectual who preaches and practices his doctrine. Are there echoes of this renaissance Mqhayi figure when, years later, in 1994, Mandela exhorted Africa to believe in itself?

> We know it is a matter of fact that we have it in our-
> selves as Africans to change all this. We must, in ac-
> tion, say that there is no obstacle big enough to stop
> us from bringing about a new African renaissance.[24]

Since the 1994 call, Thabo Mbeki has further elaborated on this theme. And his 1996 address, *"I am an African"*—with its poetic suggestiveness and its depiction of this "African" as containing in himself multitudes, a truly renaissance persona— has justifiably become a classic. Clearly, the African renaissance seems an idea whose time has come: Witness the number of books and articles and conferences[25] it has generated. The academic discussions have been rich in their economic, political, and even cultural explorations of meaning and implications of the idea. However, recent such discussions, as opposed to those that occurred during the times of Mqhayi and Vilakazi, have been virtually silent about the relationship between language and renaissance. Language, though often seen as a product and reflection of economic, political, and cultural order, is itself a material force of the highest order. It is interesting that Marx and Engels in "German Ideology" describe the entire process of production as a language, the language of real life.[26] In the same text, they describe language itself as practical consciousness.[27]

That is why we must ask: Is an African renaissance possible when we keepers of memory have to work outside our own linguistic memory? And within the prisonhouse of European linguistic memory? Often drawing from our own experiences and history to enrich the already very rich European memory? If we think of the intelligentsia as generals in the intellectual army of Africa including footsoldiers, can we expect this army to conquer when its generals are captured and held prisoner? And it is worse when they revel in their fate as captives.

In 1948, bothered by Africa's intellectuals' almost religious attachment to that European memory, Cheikh Anta Diop, another multi-talented figure in the Mqhayi tradition, posed the same question in a paper published in *Le Musée Vivant* under the title *"When Can We Talk of an African Renaissance?"* After reviewing the complex predicament of Africans writing in European languages, he ended up echoing Vilakazi's sentiments in very emphatic terms—in fact, asserting that "[i]t is absolutely indispensable to destroy this attachment to the prestige of European languages in the greater interest of Africa." He went on to say:

> Some could raise the objection that Africans who use
> foreign languages do so in an original manner and that

their expression contains something specific of their race. But what the African can never express, until he abandons the use of foreign languages, is the peculiar genius of his own languages.... [A]ll these reasons—and many more—lead me into affirming that the development of our indigenous languages is the prerequisite for a real African renaissance.[28]

Nadine Gordimer expressed similar sentiments in her contribution to a UNESCO Symposium in Harare in 1992, a paper titled "Turning the Page: African Writers in the Twenty-First Century." Here, she acknowledged, and rightly so, the brilliance of what has already been produced by African writers in acquired European tongues. Then she added:

But we writers cannot speak of taking up the challenge of a new century for African literature unless writing in African languages becomes the major component of the continent's literature. Without this, one cannot speak of an African literature. It must be the basis of the cultural cross-currents that will both buffer and stimulate that literature.[29]

What Diop[30] and Gordimer say about such literature applies to intellectual production as a whole, for renaissance is not about literature alone but, rather, entails exploration of the frontiers in the whole realm of economy, politics, science, and arts as well as the extension of dreams and imagination. Still, the quest for knowledge is central in the enterprise.

The European Renaissance involved not only exploration of new frontiers of thought but also a reconnection with Europeans' memory, the roots of which lay in ancient Greece and Rome. In practice, this reconnection involved disengagement from the tyranny of hegemonic Latin and discovery of Europeans' own tongues. But it also required a massive and sustained translation and transfer of knowledge from Latin and Greek into the emerging European vernaculars, including English. A great deal of intervernacular translation of current intellectual production also took place among the then-emerging European languages—for instance, from French into English and vice versa.

The African keepers of memory could do worse than usefully borrow a leaf from that experience. Indeed, Thabo Mbeki's contribution to the debate takes the form of a challenge to the African intelligentsia, the keepers of memory, to "add to the strengthening of the movement for Africa's renaissance."[31]

The challenge to the intelligentsia is as it should be. No renaissance can come out of state legislation and admonitions. States and governments can, should, and must provide an enabling democratic environment and resources. In this respect South Africa has to be commended for coming up with a very enlightened language policy. Most governments tend to hide their heads in the sand and pretend that African languages do not exist, or else try to force a retrograde policy of monolingualism. Governments can help by creating policies that make African languages part of the languages of social mobility and power, currently a monopoly of European languages. Ultimately, however, renaissance, as rebirth and flowering, can spring only from the wealth of imagination of the people—and, above all, from Africa's keepers of memory.

We must hearken to Vilakazi's call when he tells us to use our languages as vehicles for "thought, feeling and will."[32] We must produce knowledge in African languages and then use translation as a means of conversation in and among African languages. We must also translate from European and Asian languages into our own, for our languages must not remain isolated from the mainstream of progressive human thought in the languages and cultures of the globe. But how can we resolve our present predicament, whereby considerable knowledge produced by sons and daughters of Africa is already stored in European linguistic granaries? A lot of these works, as Gordimer has noted, are brilliant examples of the results of acquisition of European languages. Diop has repeatedly made the point that he is not underestimating the contributions by those African writers who use foreign languages. And Vilakazi in his debate with H.I.E. Dhlomo did not question the quality of Dhlomo's work. These works, like stolen gems, must be retrieved and returned to the languages and cultures that initially inspired them. The task of restoration is at the heart of the Renaissance Project.

What is the Restoration Project? As noted earlier, much of the intellectual production by the native keepers of memory in Africa has been in languages other than those of the cultures of the writers' birth and upbringing. In reality, this outcome often involves an act of cultural translation from the subject memory into the dominant memory. What does it mean when, for instance, an African writes a novel in which the peasantry and working class are the actors? Although in real life the characters would be speaking in an African language, they emerge in the novel as English, French, or Portuguese speakers. The translation that takes place in the mind of the writer before it is in black and white on a page results in the loss of that from which it is translated. Restoration would mean translating Europhone literature and Europhone intellectual productions back into the languages and cultures from which the writers have drawn. This would help to restore the works to their original languages and cultures—akin to rescuing "the original" mental text from a Europhone exile—as well as to reverse the brain drain by ensuring that the products of that brain drain return to build the original base. But restoration also has an even bigger potential: An African writer's work could be restored to all African languages. Wole Soyinka, Chinua Achebe, Alex la Guma, Pepetela, Mafouz, Tsitsi Dangarembga, and Ama Ata Aidoo could become a common heritage in all African languages. I am not talking about a new project: This process has already started. Some of Wole Soyinka's plays have been translated into Yoruba. Many works by African writers have been translated into Kiswahili, and in this respect Henry Chakava of the East African Education Publishers has led the way. The success of such restoration would depend on a creative partnership among the writer, the translator, and publisher, and the government. But such a partnership should be a conscious Africa-wide movement, an Africa restoration project calling for a grand alliance of publishers, translators, financiers, and governments.

Since the dismemberment of Africa into continent and diaspora, there has been talk of the right of return of diasporic Africans. Liberia and Sierra Leone, which were founded on that principle, produced one of the great theoreticians of the "African idea," Edward Blyden. Garvey voiced the necessity of return in the early part of the twentieth century. The most famous physical return was that of the greatest proponent of the "African idea," W.E.B. Dubois, whose burial home is

Ghana. But the farthest-reaching return would be that of the spiritual heritage created by people of African descent all over the world. This return of the spirit would be effected through translations into African languages. Such recovery was begun by the Xhosa poet J.J.R. Lolobe, who translated Booker T. Washington's *Up from Slavery* into IsiXhosa in the 1950s. But the recovery calls for more than the translation of one text by one author. It needs to be a major project throughout years to come. Afro-Caribbean and African-American thought translated into African languages would be a monumental spiritual return comparable in impact to that of Europe's recovery of its classical heritage. From Martin Delany and Olaudah Equiano to Toni Morrison, Sonia Sanchez, and Amiri Baraka; from Booker T. Washington to W.E.B. Dubois; from C.L.R. James to George Lamming and Kamau Brathwaite—if translated into African languages the works by these authors would create a shared heritage across the continent and diaspora. In time, translations of what is produced in the diaspora would become routine, part of an ongoing remembering practice.

Africa is, has been, and will always be part of the world. It's just that the continent's relationship to the world has thus far been that of donor to the West. Africa has given her human beings, her resources, and even her spiritual products through Africans writing in European languages. We should strive to do it the other way around: Have the best writings of the world—in science, philosophy, technology, and literature— translated into African languages. Africans should bring the intellectual production in the world into our native speech with all the enthusiasm of conquest.

Here, in this time and age, we may want to reexamine the role of European languages. In the past, European languages have enabled the global visibility of many writers, but they have done so by uprooting many of those writers from their own languages and cultures. They have enabled visibility in European languages and invisibility in African languages. But given that there are few people who know more than one African language, translations between two African lan- guages would have to go through a third party—which in turn would usually entail European languages. In such a sit- uation we should be using European languages to enable without disabling.

If performed on all these fronts, mutual exchange among African languages, recovery from the diaspora, and recoup- ing our share from the world would make translation an act of patriotism, a central re-membering practice within the re- membering vision of Greater Pan-Africanism.

All this calls for a very different attitude toward our lan- guages on the part of African governments and the African in- telligentsia, as once articulated by Vilakazi and Diop and exemplified by Mqhayi and the whole line of African intellectuals who have always kept faith in African languages. There are signs of positive responses to Mqhayi's call.

Some governments have begun to come up with positive policies on African languages, the prime example once again being South Africa. There are a few countries—Ethiopia, for instance—where writing and intellectual production in African languages have always been taken as the norm. The government's attitude toward culture in general and African languages in particular is critical, for, as Gordimer has rightly observed, "in the twentieth century of political struggles, state money has gone into guns, not books. As for literacy, as long as people can read state decrees and the graffiti that defy them, that has been regarded as sufficient proficiency."[33] That of course is decidedly not the best recipe for a renaissance. The state can provide an enabling environment, ensuring respect and protection of what Gordimer calls the implicit role of writers—to supply a critique of society for the greater understanding and enrichment of life. But ultimately the work of intellectual rejuvenation must come from the keepers of memory, from whom there have been encouraging signs, best exemplified by the *Asmara Declaration on African Languages and Literatures* in the year 2000, which called on African languages to accept the challenge, the duty, and the responsibility of speaking for the continent. These trends are in keeping with what seems to me the main challenge of Biko's life, thought, and legacy: to disengage ourselves from the tyranny of the European postrenaissance memory and seize back the right and the initiative to name the world by reconnecting to our memory. This returns us to the words of Nelson Mandela, that great African sage who stood in Tunis, hearing in his mind the words of the Roman general who sentenced the African city of Carthage to death, and refused to moan about the death and past loss, but instead let its memory carry him onto new waves of optimism. "All human civilization rests on the foundation of such as the ruins of the African City of Carthage,"[34] Mandela said, undoubtedly recalling all the ruins wrought on the psyche of the continent by the more contemporary empires of European modernity. Then he issued the call:

> One epoch with its historic task has come to an end. Surely another must commence with its own challenges. Africa cries out for a new birth. Carthage awaits the restoration of its glory.[35]

Surely with his life Mandela has earned the right to issue that call to the youth of Africa.

Biko would have understood that call. His life and thought—like those of Chris Hani, Robert Sobukwe, Ruth First, and all political prisoners—remind us that whatever gains have been achieved, including independence and national liberation, did not arise by themselves. They were the results of struggle and sacrifice, and it behooves us, the inheritors of any and every benefit of those sacrifices, never to forget. A people without memory are in danger of losing their soul.

Is the task in front of us, that of the recovery of the African historical memory and dreams, too difficult a task? There is no way out of this. Keepers of African memory must do for their languages what all others in history have done for theirs. As we set about disengaging from the hegemonic tyranny of bourgeois Western memory and reconnecting with that contained in the living matter of our languages, let the words of Thabo Mbeki echo determination in our hearts and not waver in our resolve:

> Whoever we may be, whatever our immediate interest, however much we carry baggage from our past, however much we have been caught by the fashion of cynicism and loss of faith in the capacity of the people, let us say—nothing can stop us now.[36]

Biko's black consciousness was all about restoring faith in the capacity of the people to reject all value systems and practices that sought to reduce their basic human dignity and make them foreigners in their own land. Rooted in positive self-affirmation, his vision was for a nonracist, just, and egalitarian society in which color and race would not be the primary point of reference.

Among the writers whom Biko admired was Aimé Césaire, whose poem *"Return to My Native Land"* is a poignant
call and celebration of a return to the sources of one's being, a vital reconnection with memory. The poem sums up
the very essence of black consciousness as an integral part
of social consciousness for a more equal human society.

> *for it is not true that the work of man*
>   *is finished*
> *that man has nothing more to do in the*
>   *world but be a parasite in the world*
> *that all we now need is to keep in step*
>   *with the world*
> *but the work of man is only just beginning*
>   *and it remains to man to conquer all*
>   *the violence embedded in the recesses*
>   *of his passion*
> *and no race possesses the monopoly of beauty,*
>   *of intelligence, of force, and there*
>   *is a place for all at the rendezvous*
>   *of victory. . . .* [37]

We can add to this by saying that no language has a monopoly as keeper of memory, and that all memories contribute to
the meeting point of human victory.

ACKNOWLEDGMENTS

I would like to thank Professor Skip Gates for inviting me to give the 2006 McMillan-Stewart Lectures at Harvard. I am also indebted to Professor Abiola Irele, Hamilton Dane, and the staff of the university for hosting me. In addition, I would like to thank Professor Gaby Schwab, Professor Jane Newman, Professor Laura O'Connor, Professor Alex Galley, and Professor Doug Pfeiffer, to whom I often turned for suggestions on further readings and discussions. My students—Robert Colson, Aisling Aboud, and Michelle Bishop—also contributed to my research, and I want to thank them for their help and take on the Irish situation. Colette Atkinson contributed ideas toward the title. Barbara Caldwell, my assistant and editor, never tired of running to the library and bookshop, or scouring the Internet, for books and references urgently needed. Laura O'Connor's *Haunted English* and

Ntongela Masilela's work on the intellectual history of South Africa were particularly inspiring. Ntongela additionally read over the lectures and came up with challenging comments and helpful suggestions. And special thanks to my wife, Njeeri, and my family for their support.

NOTES

CHAPTER ONE

1. First McMillan-Stewart Lecture at Harvard University, March 14, 2006.

2. There are numerous references to this sequence of events in the works of Adam Smith, Karl Marx, Eric Williams, C.L.R. James, and W.E.B. Dubois.

3. V. Y. Mudimbe, *The Idea of Africa* (Indiana University Press/James Currey, 1994), p. xii.

4. Christopher Marlowe, *Tamburlaine the Great, Part II* (*1587*), Act 5, Scene 3.

5. Daniel Defoe, *Robinson Crusoe* (1719) (NAL/Penguin, 1961), p. 213.

6. Ibid., p. 203.

7. For my discussion of Spenser I am indebted to Professor Laura O'Connor, who allowed me to read her doctoral dissertation. That work is now a book, *Haunted English: The Celtic Fringe, the British Empire, and De-Anglicization* (Johns Hopkins University Press, 2006).

8. Edmund Spenser, *A View of the Present State of Ireland*, edited by W. L. Renwick (Oxford University Press, 1970).

9. O'Connor, *Haunted English*, p. 3.

10. Spenser, *A View of the Present State of Ireland*, pp. 155–156.

11. Ibid., p. 156.

12. Ibid., p. 1.

13. Ibid., p. 64.

14. Ibid.

15. "This famous document, known as the Regimento of 1512, can perhaps be described as the first essay in neo-colonialism," writes Kwame Nkrumah in *Challenge of the Congo* (Nelson, 1967), pp. 2–3.

16. Page DuBois, *Torture and Truth* (Routledge, 1991).

17. T. S. Eliot, "What the Thunder Said," in *The Wasteland*.

18. Nicholas Ostler, *Empires of the Word: A Language History of the World* (HarperCollins Publishers, 2005), p. xix.

19. Ibid., p. 67.

20. Ibid.

21. Tove Skutnabb-Kanga, *Linguistic Genocide in Education* (Lawrence Erlbaum Associates, 2000). Kanga contrasts linguicide with other types of language disappearance such as language endangerment and language death.

22. Ibid., p. 369.

23. Henry Louis Gates, Jr., "Introduction: Narration and Cultural Memory in the African-American Tradition," in *Talk That Talk: An Anthology of African-American Storytelling*, edited by Linda Goss and Marian E. Barnes (Simon and Schuster, 1989), p. 15.

24. Ibid.

25. Ibid.

26. Spenser, *A View of the Present State of Ireland*, p. 104.

27. Frantz Fanon, *Black Skin, White Masks*, translated by Richard Philcox (Grove Press, 2008), p. 2.

28. Walter Benjamin, "Excavation and Memory," *Selected Writings*, Vol. 2: *1927–1934*, translated by Rodney Livingstone and others; edited by Michael W. Jennings, Howard Eiland, and Gary Smith (Belnap Press of Harvard University Press, 1999), p. 576. I am indebted to Alex Galley for drawing my attention to this piece, which was written in 1935.

29. Spenser, *A View of the Present State of Ireland*, pp. 158–159.

30. Cheikh Hamidou Kane, *Ambiguous Adventure*, translated by Katherine Woods (Walker and Company, 1963), p. 49. Also quoted in Ngũgĩ wa Thiong'o, *Decolonising the Mind: The Politics of Language in African Literature* (Heinemann, 1986), p. 9.

31. Thomas Macaulay, "Minute on Indian Education," Bill Ashcroft, Gareth Griffiths, and Helen Tiffin, eds., *The Post-Colonial Studies Reader* (Routledge, 1995), p. 430.

32. W.E.B. Dubois, *The Negro* (Dover Publications, 2001), p. 6.

33. Ben Jonson, *The Complete Masques*, edited by Stephen Orgel (Yale University Press, 1969), p. 53.

34. Ibid., p. 56.

35. Okot p'Bitek, *Song of Lawino and Song of Ocol* (Heinemann, 1984), p. 126.

36. V. Y. Mudimbe, *The Idea of Africa*, p. 129. The entirety of chapter 4, "Domestication and the Conflict of Memories," is pertinent to the question of conflict between Europhone and African memories.

37. George Lamming, *In the Castle of My Skin* (University of Michigan Press, 1991), p. 27.

CHAPTER TWO

1. Second McMillan-Stewart Lecture at Harvard University, March 15, 2006.

2. *Mūtiiri* (volume 1, issue 2). The Gīkūyū word *therera* (flow) is also evocative of cleansing and clarity.

3. Ibid.; author's (Wachira's own) translation.

4. There are many versions of the Osiris saga. The summary here is based largely on Anthony S. Mercatante's *Who's Who in Egyptian Mythology* (Crown Publishers, 1978), p. 114.

5. Marcus Garvey, *The Philosophy and Opinions of Marcus Garvey, or, Africa for the Africans,* Vol. 2, compiled by Amy Jacques-Garvey (Arno Press, 1969), p. 127.

6. Ibid., pp. 25–26.

7. Hakim Adi and Marika Sherwood, *The 1945 Manchester Pan-African Congress Revisited* (New Beacon Press, 1998), p. 56. Also quoted in Ngũgĩ wa Thiong'o, *Writers in Politics,* rev. ed. (James Currey, 1997), p. 153.

8. W.E.B. Dubois, *Dusk of Dawn: An Essay Toward an Autobiography of a Race Concept* (Harcourt, Brace, and Company, 1940), p. 116.

9. A prefatory note to the 2001 reissue of *The Negro* by Dover Publications indicates that Dubois wrote this to counter disparaging views on Africa like those expressed on the floor of the Senate by Senator James K. Vardaman. On February 6, 1914; Vardaman claimed that the black man "has never had any civilization except that which has been inculcated by a superior race. It is lamentable that his civilization lasts only so long as he is in the hands of the white man who inculcates it. When left to himself he has universally gone back to the barbarism of the jungle."

10. Molefi Kete Asante, *The Afrocentric Idea* (Temple University Press, 1998), p. xii.

11. Léopold Senghor, "Prayer to the Masks," in *The Penguin Book of African Poetry,* edited by Gerald Moore and Ulli Beier (Penguin Books, 1998), p. 316.

12. Ibid., "The Night of Sine," p. 314.

13. Frantz Fanon, *The Wretched of the Earth,* translated by Constance Farrington (Grove Press, 1963), p. 210.

14. See Nuala Ni Dhomhnaill, *Selected Essays* (New Island Books, 2005).

15. W. B. Yeats, "The De-Anglicising of Ireland," in *Yeats' Poetry, Drama and Prose,* edited by James Pethica (Norton, 2000), p. 261.

16. Ibid.

17. Ibid.

18. Ibid., p. 262.

19. Ibid.

20. Dhomhnaill, *Selected Essays,* pp. 14–15.

21. Ibid., p. 14.

22. Countee Cullen, *On These I Stand* (Harper and Row, 1947), p. 24.

23. Quoted in Henry Louis Gates, Jr., ed., *The Classic Slave Narratives* (Penguin, 1987), p. 16.

24. Ibid., p. 14.

25. George Lamming, *Pleasures of Exile* (M. Joseph, 1960), p. 224.

26. C.L.R. James, *The Black Jacobins; Toussaint L'Ouverture and the San Domingo Revolution* (Vintage Books, 1989).

27. Zora Neale Hurston, "Characteristics of Negro Expression," in *The Sanctified Church* (Turtle Island Foundation, 1983), p. 51. For this observation, I am also indebted to Aisling Cormack Aboud, "Folklore Still in the Making: Narrative Negotiations," which is cited in Hurston's *Mules and Men* as an unpublished manuscript.

28. Kamau Brathwaite, *The Arrivants* (Oxford University Press, 1973), pp. 265–266.

29. Ibid., pp. 269–270.

30. Chinua Achebe, *Arrow of God* (Anchor Books, 1974).

31. Aimé Césaire, *Discourse on Colonialism,* translated by Joan Pinkham (Monthly Review, 1972), p. 84.

32. Ibid., p. 83.

33. Matthew Arnold, *The Study of Celtic Literature (1905)* (Kennikat Press, 1970), p. 10.

34. Ibid., p. 11.

35. "What the French call the science des origins, the science of origins—a science at the bottom of all real knowledge of the actual world, and which is everyday growing in interest and importance—is very incomplete without a thorough critical account of the Celts, and their genius, language and literature." See ibid., pp. 13–14.

36. Yeats, "The De-Anglicising of Ireland," p. 262.

37. Dhomhnaill, *Selected Essays,* p. 14.

38. Fanon, *The Wretched of the Earth,* p. 153.

39. J. H. Nketia, *Funeral Dirges of the Akan People* (Negro Universities Press, 1969), p. 5.

40. Ibid., p. 6.

41. Nicolas Abraham and Maria Torok, "Mourning and Melancholia" in *The Shell and the Kernel: Renewals of Psychoanalysis,* translated by Nicholas T. Rand (University of Chicago Press, 1994), p. 130.

42. Ibid.

43. Gabriele Schwab, "Writing Against Memory and Forgetting," unpublished manuscript.

44. Ibid.

45. Ibid.

46. *Mūtiiri,* (volume 1, issue 2); author's translation.

47. Abraham and Torok, "Mourning and Melancholia," p. 104.

48. Nketia, *Funeral Dirges of the Akan People,* p. 1.

49. Schwab, "Writing Against Memory and Forgetting."

50. Zora Neale Hurston, *A Life in Letters,* edited by Carla Kaplan (Anchor Books, 2005), pp. 518–520.

51. Kofi Anyidoho, "Hero and Thief," in *The Penguin Book of African Poetry,* edited by Gerald Moore and Ulli Beier (Penguin Books, 1998), p. 130.

CHAPTER THREE

1. Third McMillan-Stewart Lecture at Harvard University, March 16, 2006.

2. Brenda Shildgene, Sander Gilman, and Gay Zhou, eds., *Introduction to Other Renaissances* (Pelgrave-McMillan, 2006).

3. Ibid.

4. Jacob Burckhardt, *The Civilization of the Renaissance in Italy* (Harper Torchbooks, 1958). Burckhardt saw the period as the first surging of a new age—a concept also attributed to the nineteenth-century French historian Jules Michelet.

5. Walter Rodney, *How Europe Underdeveloped Africa* (Howard University Press, 1974).

6. V. Y. Mudimbe, *The Idea of Africa* (Indiana University Press, 1994), p. xi.

7. On the continent, the ideas of Crummwell, Washington, Garvey, and Dubois often collapsed into the idea of the African. Kwame Nkrumah claimed equal influence from Dubois and Garvey.

8. Ntongela Masilela's massive study of the intellectual history of South Africa is a scholarly mine of information. See, for instance, his essay titled "The Transatlantic Connections of the New African Movement" (unpublished manuscript).

9. Ibid.

10. Hakim Adi and Marika Sherwood, *The 1945 Manchester Pan-African Congress Revisited* (New Beacon Press, 1995), p. 56. Also quoted in Ngũgĩ wa Thiong'o, *Writers in Politics,* rev. ed. (James Currey, 1997), p. 153.

11. David Diop, "Africa," in *The Penguin Book of African Poetry,* edited by Gerald Moore and Ulli Beier (Penguin Books, 1998), p. 328.

12. *The Portable Renaissance Reader,* edited by James Bruce Ross and Mary Martin McLaughlin (Viking Press, 1968), p. 1.

13. Karl Marx and Friedrich Engels, *The Communist Manifesto* (1848).

14. Frantz Fanon, *The Wretched of the Earth,* translated by Constance Farrington (Grove Press, 1963), p. 153.

15. Erich Auerbach, *Literary Language and Its Public in Late Latin Antiquity and in the Middle Ages,* translated by Ralph Manheim (Princeton University Press, 1993), p. 319.

16. Ibid., p. 269.

17. Robert S. Haller, trans. and ed., *Literary Criticism of Dante Alighieri* (University of Nebraska Press, 1973), ch. 1, p. 4.

18. Ibid., ch. 9, p. 13.

19. Ibid., p. 65.

20. Ibid., p. 145.

21. Quoted in John Hale, *The Civilization of Europe in the Renaissance* (Simon & Schuster, 1995), p. 156.

22. See Richard Foster Jones, *The Triumph of the English Language* (Oxford University Press, 1953).

23. This poem, by Samuel Daniel, is quoted in ibid., pp. 184–185, as well as in Hale, *The Civilization of Europe in the Renaissance,* p. 160.

24. Quoted in Hale, *The Civilization of Europe in the Renaissance*, p. 190.

25. F. O. Matthiessen, *Translation: An Elizabethan Art* (Octagon Books, 1965), p. 54.

26. Quoted in ibid., p. 181.

27. Ibid.

28. Jane O. Newman, *Pastoral Conventions: Poetry, Language, and Thought in Seventeenth-Century Nuremberg* (Johns Hopkins University Press, 1990), p. 117.

29. Quoted in *Translation—Theory and Practice: A Historical Reader*, edited by Daniel Weissbort and Astadur Eysteinsson (Oxford University Press, 2006), p. 70.

30. Newman, *Pastoral Conventions*, p. 116. The author says this of Martin Luther, but her remark would also apply to translations of the bible into the vernacular.

31. Matthiessen, *Translation: An Elizabethan Art*, p. 3.

32. Ibid.

33. Ntongela Masilela, "Themes and Categories of the New African Movement," paper presented to the Human Sciences Research Council, November 2005.

34. Guybon Bundlwana Sinxo, *The Bantu World* [South Africa], July 20, 1935. (Sinxo was the editor of the Xhosa section of *Bantu World*, a newspaper devoted to African issues.) Quoted in Masilela's paper, "Themes and Categories of the New African Movement."

35. Plato, "Cratylus," in *Plato's Collected Works*, translated by B. Jowett (Princeton University Press, 1994), p. 444.

36. Marcus Garvey, *The Philosophy and Opinions of Marcus Garvey*, Vol. 2, edited by Amy Jacques Garvey (Arno Press, 1969), pp. 25–26.

CHAPTER FOUR

1. This chapter is based on the Fourth Steve Biko Annual Lecture, which I gave at Cape Town University in Cape Town, South Africa, on September 12, 2003. In the writing of it I am indebted to the work of Dr. Ntongela Masilela and to the discussions I had with him over the intellectual tradition in South Africa.

2. Quoted from Nelson Mandela's speech, "Statement at OAU Heads of States Meeting" in Tunis, June 13, 1994; available online at http://www.anc.org.za/ancdocs/history/mandela/1994/.

3. Steve Biko, *I Write What I Like* (Ravan Press, 1996), p. 153. (Reprinted in 2000.)

4. Nelson Mandela's statement from the dock at the opening of the defense case in the Rivonia Trial, Pretoria Supreme Court, April 20, 1964.

5. Engraved on the commemorative stone outside the house in which Biko grew up, in Ginsberg, South Africa.

6. Robert Sobukwe, address on behalf of the 1949 graduating class at Fort Hare College, delivered at the "Completers' Social."

7. On the roots of Ethiopianism, a kind of African nationalism in Christian robes. This theme can be seen in biblical texts such as the thirty-first verse of the sixtieth Psalm: *"Ethiopia shall soon stretch out her hands to God."* On the Abyssinian defeat of the Italians in Adowa in 1896 as well as on African-American Independent Church movements, see George Shepperson and Thomas Price, *Independent African: John Chilembwe and the Origins, Setting and Significance of the Nyasaland Native Rising of 1915* (Edinburgh University Press, 1958), p. 72. (Reprinted in 1963.)

8. Thabo Mbeki, *Africa: The Time Has Come* (Tafelberg/ Mafube, 1998). "I am an African" was part of the deputy

president's Statement on Behalf of the ANC, delivered at the time of the adoption of South Africa's 1996 Constitution Bill, Cape Town, May 1996.

9. Now reproduced in my book *Moving the Center* (James Currey Ltd., 1993) under the chapter title "Resistance to Damnation: The Role of Intellectual Workers."

10. See "Many Years Walk to Freedom: Welcome Home Mandela!" in my *Moving the Center.*

11. Smith's core arguments can be found in this seminal work, an edition of which was published in 1991 by Prometheus Books.

12. Paul Le Blanc, *From Marx to Gramsci* (Humanities Press International, 1996), pp. 128–129.

13. Ibid., p. 131.

14. C.L.R. James, *The Black Jacobins: Toussaint L'Ouverture and the San Domingo Revolution* (Vintage Books, 1989), p. 283.

15. Biko, *I Write What I Like*, p. vi.

16. Shepperson and Price, *Independent African*, pp. 71, 77. More work needs to be done to unearth the histories of Dinizulu on Napoleon's island of St. Helena.

17. "Of all modern languages, English is the noblest, fullest, deepest, and most comprehensive. We natives of this country receive with thanks every inducement to learn that language. It is the language of the Arts and Sciences, the language of the Law and Politics. It is the channel to all the benefits of civilization. . . . Another use of this society will be to unite the different native tribes of this country by the English language and manners." See Gwayi Tyamzashe, "A Native Society at Kimberley," *The Christian Express*, April 1, 1884; quoted in Ntongela Masilela, "An Intellectual History of the New African Movement," unpublished manuscript. Bear in mind that, although the role of English crops up in many debates about the regeneration of the

country, many South African intellectuals were also specialists in their own African languages and did not disparage their use.

18. B. W. Vilakazi, Letter to the Editor, *The South African Outlook,* July 1, 1939.

19. Ibid.

20. Ibid. This statement precedes that of Obi Wali, who in the 1960s took a similar position on African writing in European languages. (See *Transition,* Vol. 10.)

21. Ibid.

22. Nelson Mandela, *Long Walk to Freedom* (Little, Brown, 1995), p. 41.

23. Ibid.

24. Quoted on the African National Congress website at http://www.anc.org.za/ancdocs/history/mandela/1994/.

25. In particular, see the text of Mbeki's speeches in *Africa: The Time Has Come* (Tafelberg/Mafube, 1998) and *Africa: Define Yourself* (Tafelberg/Mafube, 2002). See also *The African Renaissance* (May 1998), with articles by Thabo Mbeki, Mangosuthu Buthelezi, Sean Michael Cleary, Francis A. Kornegay and Chris Landsberg, and Yvonne Mokgoro; Washington A. J. Okumu, *The African Renaissance: History, Significance, and Strategy* (Africa World Press, 2002); Fantu Cheru, *African Renaissance: Roadmaps to the Challenge of Globalization* (Palgrave, 2002); Moyo Okediji, *African Renaissance: New Forms, Old Images in Yoruba Art* (University Press of Colorado, 2002); *Black Renaissance/ Renaissance Noire,* a quarterly journal edited by the Institute of African-American Affairs at New York University; Mukanda M. Mulenfo, *Thabo Mbeki and the African Renaissance: The Emergence of a New African Leadership* (Actua Press, 2000); Malegapuru William Makgoba, ed., *African Renaissance: The New Struggle* (Mafube/

Tafelberg, 1999); and Cheikh Anta Diop, *Towards the African Renaissance: Essays in African Culture and Development 1946–1960*, translated from the French by Egbuna P. Modum (Karnac House, 1996). It is interesting that these essays previously issued under a different title are now so titled in the 1996 Karnac House and Red Sea Press editions. Leonard Barnes's *African Renaissance* (Bobbs-Merrill, 1969) does not belong to the current revival.

26. "The production of ideas, of conceptions, of consciousness, is at first directly interwoven with the material activity and the material intercourse of men—the language of real life." See Karl Marx and Frederick Engels, "German Ideology," in *Collected Works*, Vol. 5: *Marx and Engels: 1845–47* (Progress Publishers, 1976), p. 36.

27. "The 'mind' is from the outset afflicted with the curse of being 'burdened' with matter, which here makes its appearance in the form of agitated layers of air, sounds, in short, of language. Language is as old as consciousness, language is practical, real consciousness that exists for other men as well, and only therefore does it exist for me: language, like consciousness, only arises from the need, the necessity, of intercourse with other men." See ibid., pp. 43–44.

28. Cheikh Anta Diop, *Towards the African Renaissance*, p. 35. The translation from the French is by Egbuna P. Modum.

29. Now reprinted in Nadine Gordimer, *Living in Hope and History: Notes from Our Century* (Farrar, Straus and Giroux, 1999), p. 34.

30. See Cheikh Anta Diop, "A Continent in Search of Its History," in *Towards the African Renaissance*. Of particular interest in this context is the author's discussion of the capacities of African languages for thought and science.

31. Thabo Mbeki, Preface to *African Renaissance: The New Struggle,* edited by Malegapuru William Makgoba (Mafube/Tafelberg, 1999).

32. Vilakazi, Letter to the Editor. See also Diop, "A Continent in Search of Its History."

33. Gordimer, *Living in Hope and History,* p. 35.

34. Quoted on the African National Congress website at http://www.anc.org.za/ancdocs/history/mandela/1994/.

35. Ibid.

36. Mbeki, *Africa: The Time Has Come,* p. 36.

37. Quoted in C.L.R. James, *The Black Jacobins* (Vintage 1989), p. 401.

INDEX

158 INDEX